A GRAVE AT
GLORIETA

The Harrison Raines Civil War Mysteries
by Michael Kilian

A GRAVE AT GLORIETA

A HARRISON RAINES CIVIL WAR MYSTERY

Michael Kilian

BERKLEY PRIME CRIME, NEW YORK

This is a work of fiction. Names, characters, places, and incidents either
are the product of the author's imagination or are used fictitiously,
and any resemblance to actual persons, living or dead, business
establishments, events, or locales is entirely coincidental.

A GRAVE AT GLORIETA

A Berkley Prime Crime Book
Published by The Berkley Publishing Group,
a division of Penguin Putnam Inc.,
375 Hudson Street, New York, New York 10014.

Visit our website at
www.penguinputnam.com

Copyright © 2003 by Michael Kilian.
Jacket art by Tony Greco & Associates, Inc.

First edition: January 2003

Library of Congress Cataloging-in-Publication Data

Kilian, Michael, 1939–
    A grave at Glorieta : a Harrison Raines Civil War mystery / Michael
Kilian.— 1st ed.
        p.   cm.
    ISBN 0-425-18829-9
    1. Raines, Harrison (Fictitious character)—Fiction.   2. New
Mexico—History—Civil War, 1861–1865—Fiction.   3. Glorieta Pass,
Battle of, N.M., 1862—Fiction.   I. Title.

PS3561.I368 G73 2003
813'.54—dc21
                                                        2002026292

PRINTED IN THE UNITED STATES OF AMERICA

10   9   8   7   6   5   4   3   2   1

For my brother Joe,

in fond memory.

Acknowledgments

I am enormously indebted to my friend, David Elliott, of Santa Fe; Roger Kennedy, former director of the National Park Service; and Randy Rasmussen, of the Albuquerque office of the National Parks and Conservation Association, for helping me gain a fuller and deeper understanding of the Civil War in New Mexico and life in the Old West. I am blessed to have Gail Fortune as my editor and Dominick Abel as my literary representative, and I am grateful to my wife, Pamela, and sons, Eric and Colin, as only they can know.

Author's Note

IT is the intent of this series to use the medium of the murder mystery to bring Civil War history to life—weaving a fictional story into the fabric of actual events involving real people. The 1862 Battle of Glorieta Pass, know to historians as "The Gettysburg of the West," was a very real and highly significant event that helped keep the western territories and California in the Union and stymied Jefferson Davis's plans to acquire a blockade-free port on the Pacific. It is my hope that I have related it as it truly occurred and that my fictional characters Harrison Raines, Jacques Tantou, Isabel Almaden, and Anselmo Sabio, among others, will seem as real to the reader as Lieutenant Colonel Manuel Chavez, Major John Chivington, and others who were actually there.

Chapter 1

March 1862

THE fast British packet steamer *Elizabeth McGovern* had been blessed with fair winds and fair skies all the way down the Atlantic coast to Havana, encouraging Harry Raines in the belief that he might actually arrive on Texas soil in time to accomplish something of the mission to which he and his fellow U.S. Secret Service agent, Joseph "Boston" Leahy, had been assigned.

The side-wheeler boasted two masts and seven sail when under full canvas. After they'd picked up the easterlies off the Turtle Islands, the captain had kept every inch aloft, running before the wind all the way across the Gulf of Mexico. Impeded by only one small storm, they'd arrived off Galveston a day ahead of their expected time—but there were several hundred miles still to travel once ashore.

Though a Virginian born and raised, Harry was participating in the great Civil War on the side of the Union and in the federal Secret Service established by former Chicago railroad detective Allan Pinkerton. Harry had been sent to this hot and sticky clime to confirm reports that the Rebels were preparing an invasion of New Mexico Territory and regions farther west, a wartime expansion that it was feared might reach as far as California. He was a poor choice for the task, as even now he wasn't quite sure where Texas ended and New Mexico began. He had hitherto never been farther west than Mississippi, but Mr. Pinkerton had been pleased with his work in the East and wanted more of it now from the West.

There was haze that early morning, and the Texas port was hard to discern along the smudgy pencil line of land at the horizon—especially for Harry, who was significantly shortsighted and vain about wearing spectacles. When he wore them, he was sometimes mistaken for a schoolteacher, and once even for a clergyman. They sat upon his nose infrequently as a consequence.

Without them, he'd been pronounced a man of agreeable countenance by a number of ladies—Southern as well as Northern. He was tall, slender, regular of feature, and had sandy-colored hair, a cavalier's long moustache, and soft brown eyes. Augmenting this was a Virginia gentleman's fancy for fine clothes. In sum, he looked the man he'd been brought up to be, a planter's son from one of the largest plantations of the Virginia Tidewater. What didn't show was how much he hated the "peculiar institution" that supported that vast estate, and the arrogance of people like his own father, who had patterned their American lives after the haughty ones of the British gentry of a century before.

"Flattest place I have bloody well ever seen," said Harry's

colleague "Boston" Leahy, as they stood at the *McGovern's* rail looking at the shore.

Leahy had been a police detective in Boston and had an Irish-flavored Boston accent to match, so the sobriquet was inevitable. Near Harry's six feet in height, Leahy abstained from spirits and exercised obsessively. His muscular shoulders defied a tailor's ability to make his suit coats fit.

"It gets bumpier," Harry said. "I understand there are mountains out there three times as high as Old Rag in Virginia."

"Let us hope we get to have a look at them," Leahy said, nodding toward the Rebel steam frigate that was bearing down on them from the northwest. "Mr. Pinkerton would not be pleased to have us begin this undertaking chained in the hold of one of Jeff Davis's ships."

Harry was surprised by the aggressive approach of the warship and feared for a moment it might be a Union vessel, which would upset all their plans. He wanted to be taken for a Confederate operative, but not if it meant his arrest.

He tried to reassure himself that such a thing was no longer possible. The *McGovern* was an English vessel. The previous fall, a U.S. Navy vessel had stopped and boarded the British ship *Trent* on the high seas, taking off two London-bound Confederate diplomats at gunpoint. The incident had provoked a parliamentary outcry in London that came close to a declaration of war. At the very least, it had been feared that the seizure might lead to British recognition of the Rebel regime, a major objective of Jefferson Davis's strategy.

Britain had been striving to prevent the expansion of the United States into a continental power ever since American independence. The English had plotted and connived toward the creation of a separate North American republic in the Southwest—abetting some of the most ridiculous breakaway movements imaginable—and had almost gone to war trying to keep U.S. settlement out of the Pacific Northwest. Many of Britain's ruling class had viewed the firing on Fort Sumter as a blessed event. Only the British public's distaste for slavery was staying the hand of Their Lordships, and not by much.

But Abraham Lincoln was no fool and had defused the explosive situation by releasing the two Southern agents.

The *McGovern*'s other passengers on deck were watching the approaching ship with great interest. All were in civilian dress, though Harry suspected several were Confederate military operatives of some sort. He and Leahy had been eyed with some curiosity for much of the *McGovern*'s voyage.

Harry felt much like a man who could not swim who'd been thrown into the deepest of oceans. They'd been given the names of only three Union sympathizers who would help them—two in Texas and one up in Santa Fe in the New Mexico Territory.

Happily, there were Union forts along the upper Rio Grande and to the east of the Sangre de Cristo mountain range, offering refuge were they able to penetrate that far into New Mexico. But the garrisons would not have been informed of Harry's or Leahy's coming, and certainly not of their mission. The nearest telegraph would be in Denver City.

So the two of them would have to rely on their own resources, which in Harry's case amounted mostly to two .36 caliber Navy Colt revolvers, a derringer pocket pistol,

a sheath knife, and five hundred dollars in gold coins se-
creted in various places on his person. This, in a desolate,
inhospitable country about which he knew damned little.
Leahy—a city man before the war—knew even less.

Pinkerton had said he had chosen them because he
feared they had become too well known in the East and he
wanted them working at a far remove from the federal
capital. But in the East, Harry had succeeded at this trade
mostly because he had been on home ground. As in the
old Negro folk tale about Br'er Rabbit, it was his briar
patch. He knew most every road and river between the
Virginia Capes and the mountain ridges west of Cumber-
land, Maryland. More to the point, he had friends in all
manner of places, north and south.

Out here, most everyone they came upon would likely
be an enemy.

"Don't worry, laddy buck," said Leahy, his eyes on the
warship. "I don't think they'll be delaying us long. We'll
be in Galveston directly."

"That is what prompts my worry," Harry said. "I feel
about Texas as I might darkest Africa."

Harrison Grenville Raines had grown up among the
self-styled aristocracy that had thrived along the James
River almost since Virginia's founding as a colony. Breaking with his father over the slavery issue, he'd decamped
to Richmond and subsequently moved to Washington
City, becoming an admirer of President Lincoln even before
that man was elected. Despite these sentiments, he viewed
the war as the recourse of lunatics. He initially had intended to maintain a neutrality, at least as concerned military service.

But it quickly became the kind of war where a man

with any self-respect and conviction had no choice but to make a choice. And so he had become Captain Raines, Union Army "scout," uncomfortable as that status made him now.

The warship hove to on their port side, displaying the Stars and Bars. The other passengers seemed relieved. Harry tried to imitate them, though relief was not his feeling at all. He stepped back, standing behind a shroud as he watched the military vessel lower a longboat. It quickly filled with oarsmen and a few Rebel Marines, led by a very junior-looking officer. As the boat approached, the captain of the Confederate frigate kept its guns aimed at the *McGovern*. One seemed targeted directly on Harry's head.

He moved to the side. "I wish we were ashore."

Leahy squinted at the longboat. "I expect that once we get there, you may change your mind."

The boarding party came thumping onto the deck, then stood at attention while their officer, a very young lieutenant, approached the *McGovern*'s captain. The officers conversed briefly, then orders were given and the men, looking as though they well knew their business, dispersed and headed below decks.

Harry turned and leaned back against the rail, observing the Confederates as they went about their work. As other passengers were doing much the same, he didn't think he'd be much noticed. But the naval lieutenant abruptly concluded his conversation with the British captain and came directly over to Leahy and Harry.

"What is your name, sir?" he asked.

"Harrison Raines."

"Have you any identity papers?"

What Harry possessed in that regard was a letter from

General Robert E. Lee, recommending him as a recruit for the Confederate States Navy, and a military pass signed by President Abraham Lincoln, authorizing him to go where he wished within military jurisdictions.

He showed only the former, hoping it would not get him press ganged into the Confederate navy at this very spot. Harry had acquired the document while in Richmond on his last mission, keeping it in hopes the general's signature might be of use here on the frontier.

The young lieutenant examined the letter with unrestrained doubt.

"Who is this General Lee?"

"His Excellency President Davis's principal military advisor."

"The letter says something about the navy." Much of the writing had become smudged.

"The Confederacy is lacking in ships, so we serve where we can."

"You are in civilian clothes."

Harry looked down at his waist coat. "Yes."

"Is this letter all you have?" the officer asked.

"I have my *cartes de visite*." He produced one.

The lieutenant examined it, as though some secret code might be hidden in its lettering. Then he pocketed it.

"You reside in Richmond?"

"Yes. Well, I did."

"What are you doing out here?"

"Looking for horses—remounts for the army."

The officer glanced at Leahy, who said nothing. The lieutenant returned his attention to Harry.

"But that letter says 'navy.' "

"Easier to procure horses than ships."

"You're an American citizen?"

"Certainly."

"I mean, on the federal side?"

"I'm a Virginian, sir. Why do you ask about that?"

The lieutenant nodded back toward the British skipper. "The captain there said he thought you were a Yankee."

Harry's blood seemed to freeze. "What made him think that?"

"He said you talked kindly about President Lincoln at dinner the other night."

And so he had. He could think of no circumstance where he might speak ill of the man, though now he wondered if one might present itself if he wasn't careful.

"The good captain presumes too much from a chance remark," he said. "I am a loyal Virginian."

"Are you armed?"

"Yes. Who is not these days?"

"Indeed. Most particularly so out here."

The lieutenant smiled, turned and moved along the deck. He paused to talk with two more passengers, then went to take the report of one of the details he'd sent below, who was now returning. Before long, his entire boarding party had reassembled, apparently having found nothing worth bothering about below.

By the time the Rebel sailors were back in their long-boat, the British captain had ordered up steam.

"You're packed?" Harry asked.

"Aye," said Leahy. "Hours ago."

"I'll go ready my bag. I want to be the first one off this ship."

"As I warned you, laddy buck. You may swiftly have a change of mind."

Chapter 2

DON Luis Almaden y Cortes had been twenty-eight years old the first time the Americanos had invaded Santa Fe. He had been no admirer of General Santa Ana, the Mexican president, whom he viewed as a vain and avaricious despot. But Almaden had taken up arms and helped fight the gringos anyway, for they had been invading not only his community but his country—the Republic of Mexico—which he felt bound to defend no matter who its leader.

The first U.S. troops to appear in the city in that long ago war were regulars under General Stephen Kearny. They had easily brushed aside the local resistance, swiftly taking possession of Santa Fe and the one-story Palace of the Governors on the town plaza without a shot fired. These American soldiers, a mix of veterans and volunteers, had conducted themselves in an orderly, disciplined fashion, treating the local population with respect.

Unfortunately, they'd moved on, to take part in the United States' inexorable conquest of the richest prize in that war—California. Thereafter, in Santa Fe, and in Taos just to the north, the problem was the ragtag Texans who'd come into New Mexico in the wake of the regular army and behaved like the conquering barbarian hordes of antiquity. Two of the kitchen maids at the Almaden hacienda out in the countryside east of Santa Fe had been raped, and more than a dozen horses had been taken. At that, Almaden had considered himself fortunate.

Now, sixteen years later, the Anglos were invading again. But the New Mexico they'd ridden into had become an official territory of the United States. These gringos were self-declared foreigners—the army of a newly created and loathsome republic called the Confederate States of America. Don Luis Almaden was their enemy, a citizen of the United States.

He would resist the foreign invader once again. He had been preparing for this ever since word had arrived of the Confederates' victory over the Yankees in February, down at a Rio Grande River crossing called Valverde.

But the news that had broken that morning—that the invading Texans were now north of Albuquerque and heading straight for Santa Fe—had somehow taken him by surprise, unnerving him not a little. It was one thing to prepare for a disaster, another to actually confront it.

His coach and four-horse team were waiting outside. He was seated in the study of his sprawling adobe house, just east of Santa Fe's plaza, contemplating what remained to be done before he fled the territorial capital.

The windows behind him were open to the street, and dust was sifting inside from the inordinate amount of horse traffic moving into and out of the town. He ignored it. Placing two loaded revolvers on the desktop, he set about his business, which mostly involved going through papers he had kept in a locked lower drawer.

He set aside three letters and a map, which he folded over and placed inside the leather lining of his boot. The other papers he gathered up and took to his stone fireplace. Kneeling, he struck a match and set them afire.

There was a rapping at the door. Almaden rose, but before he could reach the desk and the pistols he'd left upon it, the door opened. It was well he'd not been able to fetch up his weapons. The intruder was only his son, Roberto.

"The soldiers are near, Father—way up the Albuquerque road. They'll be in Santa Fe by tonight."

"I know. I've been trying to find you. I need you and your brother to take some things from here, take them to safety."

The young man came nearer. "I saw the coach is outside. What things?"

Almaden nodded toward the far corner of the room, where an Indian blanket covered a large chest. "That, for one. I want it out of Santa Fe as soon as possible. I'll give you a map to show you where to go. Now, where is your brother?"

"Eduardo left for Fort Union—to join the militia."

"Without speaking with me?"

"He left at once. Said it was a long journey."

"Fort Union is on the other side of the Sangre de Cristo Mountains. Not that far." Almaden had doubts about his youngest son.

"Then he'll be there all the sooner. Shall I take Isabel with me?"

Almaden shook his head. "No, I need your sister here."

"But it will be dangerous here."

Almaden grinned. "That's why I need her." He didn't wait for his son to fathom that irony. "Do you have others you can trust? Friends? People not mixed up with the Hidalgo group?"

"Yes, I think so."

"I mean men in whose hands you would place your own life, for that is what you will be doing."

"I know one or two. Alejandro Martinez maybe."

"*Bueno*. When you've completed the task, then you can join your brother in the militia, if that is where he goes. I will try to contact you."

"You insist on staying here in Santa Fe?"

"These people must be resisted at all costs, Roberto. If we fail—and New Mexico becomes part of their country—it will be a horror beyond imagining."

"Father, they are the enemy of our enemy."

"You do not understand these Texans. If they conquer, we will be their next Negroes."

"Slaves? That's ridiculous."

"Let us hope you do not have learn how wrong you are."

"If you fear them, Father, why stay here?"

"Because here is where I can best fight them. And we are getting help. People are being sent to us from Washington. Some kind of agents. I expected them before this. Now I must wait for them." Almaden struck a match, lighting a thin cigar. "But my immediate concern is getting that chest into the coach."

"The Texans are still miles away, Father."

"And you need to be miles away when they come. So, please."

* * *

WHEN satisfied that Roberto and the coach were on the now-crowded road leading east out of town past the little fortress of Fort Marcy, Almaden took a saddle horse and rode down to the plaza. Carts, wagons, and carriages were everywhere. The dust was so thick it seemed a fog.

Turning a corner, he pulled up before a large house with a gated courtyard, one he had visited many times, many evenings, but not gone near in the last two days. Starting to dismount, he hesitated, then eased back into the saddle again.

The woman who lived there was named Mercedes. Part Spanish, part Louisiana French, she was welcome in both the Mexican and Anglo communities. A widow nearly as wealthy as he, a remarkably handsome and very strong-willed woman, she had attracted him from the first moment of their meeting, and she had responded warmly to his attentions. He feared that now there might be only cold anger.

She was a Southerner—an outspoken Secessionist. She would not be needing his protection in the coming invasion. Almaden would more likely be needing hers. But he doubted that would be forthcoming. They had quarreled—bitterly—over the war. It seemed to him they could be no more reconciled than the American nation.

Almaden moved on, returning to the long, low-roofed Palace of the Governors at a trot. Governor Connelly had already departed the city, but clerks and soldiers were still loading office files, strong boxes, and weaponry onto wagons parked in a train. Looking about for a friendly face, he noted a large, heavyset man with a dark Spanish face seated on a bench.

"Emiliano!"

The man looked up, then smiled. He rose stiffly and came up to Almaden's horse, rubbing his hip.

"I fell this morning," he said. "On my bad leg."

In the war between the gringos and Mexico, Emiliano Vasquez had been wounded at Buena Vista. He was now one of the richest men in Santa Fe, but had the look and habits of an old pensioner.

"You're staying?" Almaden asked.

"Why not?"

"How many of the others?"

He shrugged. "More than are leaving."

Almaden dismounted, then took up his horse's reins and started walking slowly toward a cantina on the other side of the plaza. "Come with me, Emiliano. We can have a drink. And talk."

The other man nodded and fell into halting step. "There is only one thing to talk about."

"Yes. But better with tequila."

ANOTHER of Almaden's friends, Don Carlos Martinez y Lomas, was already in the cantina, seated at a rear corner table with a stranger who proved to be a visitor from Mexico named Pablo Sanchez. Others came in after them. All seemed to be of the same mind. Better to greet the invaders together, presenting something of a united front.

They were mostly of like mind.

"You are right, Luis," Martinez said to Almaden. "These bastards would be happy to make slaves of us, as they did the Indians and Negroes."

"It was we Spanish who tried to enslave the Indians," Almaden said. "A cruel and unimaginably stupid notion."

"We fought the Texans in '36 because they brought slavery to Mexico," said Vasquez. "But they call us the villains of that fight—and themselves the champions of liberty. Liberty, hell."

Almaden pulled out his watch. Time was getting short. "I expect Colonel Canby and his force to come to our rescue. But it will take days, perhaps weeks. And there will be a big fight. We must help them in every way we can."

Vasquez was staring at the tabletop, thinking. There were those who fought on the side that was right, and those who fought for the side that might win.

"You must fight, too, Emiliano," he said to Vasquez.

"I intend to. We will all fight. As you know, Don Luis. As I hope you will not forget."

The cantina was the best in Santa Fe, but had little custom among the gringos, and so was favored by the ranking senors of the town and the surrounding haciendas. Before long, the barroom was filled. There were men in the room whom Almaden feared, as well as those who might give their own lives to save his. Yet here they were all friends—Mexicans, beset by gringos.

Though the American Civil War was about to burst upon all their lives, there was as always talk at Almaden's table of another such conflict under way—far to the south—in Mexico. That fratricidal war down there was in its fourth year. Forces loyal to Benito Juárez were fighting those of Mexico's great landowners and the church. Chief justice of Mexico's supreme court when the fighting began, Juárez had formed his own government in exile and made himself president. If he prevailed, he would rule the country, an outcome devoutly to be wished.

Not all of Almaden's friends in Santa Fe approved of or

supported Juárez. The man was a full-blooded Indian—the first ever to hold such power in Mexico. His liberal ideas included reform of the system of peonage. The conflict was called "the Reform War."

Juárez was supported by Abraham Lincoln. If the Confederates succeeded in the American Civil War, they would turn on Juárez—and doubtless invade Mexico. There was no good reason for any Mexican to support the American Rebel cause, though Almaden suspected some of his friends might claim kinship with the slavers. They, too, were wealthy landowners, and doubtless thought the Confederates would treat them as fellow aristocrats.

They were his friends, but they were being fools.

The door opened. It had been doing so all afternoon, but the figure who stood silhouetted against the bright daylight now was different—a beautiful young woman, her dark hair pulled tightly back and held with a crimson ribbon.

Almaden finished his tequila and rose. "Senors, I must go. I will see you this evening."

"If we are not all in jail," said Emiliano. He was drunk, and when he began to laugh, he could not stop.

On his way to the door, Almaden stopped at the table where Pablo Sanchez was drinking. He bade him stand, pulling him aside.

"I have added to your baggage, senor. It is not much. But it may help."

"*Muchas gracias*, Don Luis. It is appreciated."

"We are also giving you a better horse. The best in Santa Fe. A palomino. It is right outside."

"What can I do for you in return?"

Almaden looked to Don Carlos Martinez. "Leave soon."

* * *

ISABEL had gone back outside, and was standing at the edge of the wooden sidewalk, the hood of her cloak now pulled over her head against the wind and dust.

"He could be right," she said.

"Who?"

"Emiliano. They could arrest you."

Leading their horses, they began to walk, heading across the street and then across the plaza.

"No," he said. "They will be preoccupied with trying to find the federal army. It is afterwards, after the next battle, that they will begin to cause trouble for us."

"And if they think we know where the Yankees are?"

Almaden brushed at his hair with his hand, trying to get out the dust. There was less of it on the far side of the plaza.

"They will know where the Federals are," he said. "They have maps. Or they will get them. It will be obvious that the U.S. troops are on the other side of the Sangre de Cristo, and that they will have to go through Glorieta Pass to get to them."

"What if the Confederates ask you to fight for them?"

"They won't. No more than they would ask the Negroes to fight for them. But I am going to fight them." He looked uneasily around him, then at the gathering dusk over the eastern mountains. "First we must attend to more pressing business."

"Everything is ready. I have the wagon waiting behind the Mission of San Miguel."

"Good."

"You want no outriders?"

"No. That would attract attention. We'll go as soon as it's dark."

"When we finish—perhaps we should keep going, Father. Aunt Mariel in Taos will be happy to have us."

"No. I want to stay away from there. And I want you to go south. You and Anselmo."

"Anselmo?"

"Yes."

"Don't you need him?"

"No.

"Where will we go?"

"There are Americanos coming—sent by President Lincoln. We are to help them. Go to Peralta and wait for them, then bring them to me. If the Confederates are still here, they will need your help getting into Santa Fe."

"They are spies?"

"Spies. Agents. Not soldiers."

"How will I know them?"

"I expect that as strangers from the East they will readily make themselves known. All the message said was that there will be two of them."

"And if they are caught by the Confederates before we can get to them?"

"That will be sad, for I think they will be hanged."

Chapter 3

HARRY had found a poker game in a Galveston water-front saloon that was crowded with barflies, assorted idlers, arriving and departing travelers, sailors of several nations, some Confederate soldiers, and two sharp-eyed fellows Harry took to be either local detectives or agents for Jefferson Davis's version of Allan Pinkerton's Secret Service. They stood with their backs to the bar, keeping most everyone in the room under surveillance.

One of them of a sudden joined the game and almost immediately began asking Harry pointed questions.

"You off that British ship?" he asked. A tall, thin man, badly shaven and snake-like in countenance, he stared hard at Harry over his hand of cards, all but ignoring them.

"I am," said Harry, examining his own hand intently. He had a ten high, perhaps the worst hand he'd been dealt in all his years playing cards.

"Where're you bound?" His interrogator had the manner of a judge with a full docket of capital punishment cases, with Harry's being his very first.

"Not sure," said Harry, discarding a four of hearts and a deuce of clubs. He'd left himself a ten of spades, nine of spades, and a six of diamonds.

"You aim just to drift around Texas?"

Harry picked up the two new cards he'd been dealt. "Not drift. I'm a horse trader. Looking for mounts to send east."

"Texas's been pretty much picked over," said another of the players, a portly man with a striped vest, "unless you get on out into West Texas."

"Then that's where I'll go."

"Easy place to get yourself killed," said another player.

"The war's out there," said yet another. "Indians, too."

"The war's everywhere," Harry said. "General Lee needs fresh mounts."

"Who's General Lee?" said the portly man in the striped vest.

The bet was a dollar. Harry studied his hand once more, then saw the wager.

"I remember Lee," said another player. "He was a colonel out here with a cavalry regiment in the Union Army. Instead of joining up when Texas seceded, he went back East."

"You're buyin' mounts for the Yankee army?" said the man next to Harry.

"General Robert E. Lee," Harry intoned, slowly, "is a lieutenant general in the Confederate States army. He is principal military advisor to President Davis. Don't you get newspapers out here?"

His companions fell silent.

Harry pulled a letter from his pocket that had been signed by Lee. Though much of it had been smeared into illegibility, the signature and the official closing were clear. With a flourish, he tossed the letter in front of the hard staring man he took to be a police agent.

The fellow ignored it, his eyes still narrowed on Harry.

"Let me see that." The voice came from behind Harry. The accent was Boston Irish.

The police agent's scowl deepened. He looked over the newcomer, up and down, then shoved the letter back across the table.

Leahy reached over Harry's shoulder and fetched up the letter. "That's General Lee all right." He set down the paper again carefully, but gave it a little shove to indicate Harry should put it back in his coat pocket as quickly as possible.

"Who are you?" asked the police agent.

"I'm from Richmond," Leahy said. "And that's all you need to know."

He went to the bar and stood there with a foot on the rail. A teetotaler, he'd be ordering lemonade.

Harry gazed steadily at his hand without betraying the fact that he now held a ten-high straight. When the betting got back around to him, there was more than twenty dollars in the pot.

Hesitating, he realized that everyone at the table was now looking at him as though they suspected him of something—if only card marking.

"I fold," he said, with a sigh, dropping his cards face down on the table. He sat back, taking out his pocket watch and looking at it. "Better deal me out."

He rose and went to the bar, standing a few paces from Leahy. He ordered Old Overholtz, his favorite whiskey, but the bartender eyed him as though he'd asked for a jug full of diamonds.

"Tennessee sour mash's the best I got," he said.

"Tennessee's fine with me."

Harry sipped the liquor, savoring it, and taking note of the fact that the snake-faced Rebel detective had left the poker game and resumed his station down the bar.

Leahy finished his lemonade and asked directions to the sinks. The bartender indicated the open back door. Harry watched the Irishman make his way through the crowd in his boxer's easy fashion, then drained his glass and followed.

There were no sinks—just a shallow trench dug across the rear yard along a fence that separated it from the beach and bay beyond. Leahy was the only one there at the moment, but the trench had been much patronized.

"No reason for all this play-acting, laddy buck," he said. "We were seen together on the ship, you know."

"Then why the charade in there with Lee's letter?"

"Keep 'em off balance. I'm betting that curious son of a bitch is with the Texas government. Police agent or some such, like those 'Plug Uglies' back in the Confederate capital. In which case, he has a superior, who might not take kindly to his affronting two secret agents from Richmond who could cause trouble for the superior's superior."

"I shouldn't think the Richmond writ has much sway out here," Harry said. He stepped back from the smelly trench, thankful for the breeze from the ocean.

"Probably not," said Leahy, moving away as well. "But the lowly likes of that viper in there won't be knowin' that. And that was no charade, boyo. We are secret agents, are we not? And we were just a wee while ago in Richmond."

Harry glanced nervously at the barred rear window of the barroom. "Let's go for a walk on the beach."

"SAND here's damned near white," Leahy said, kicking it. "Not like Nantasket."

"What in hell is Nantasket?"

"A lovely spit of land south of Boston harbor. Dark sand and full of pebbles. Reminds me of the Irish coast at Lahinch."

"I've learned nothing," Harry said, changing the subject. "And our steamer for the mainland leaves within the hour."

"It's not Galveston that concerns us, Mr. Raines. I have managed to learn a wee something, such as that the game out here may already be up."

"And how is that?"

"The western part of New Mexico appears to be as Secesh as Old Virginia. It's risen up against the Union, and your friend Jeff Davis has officially declared it the Territory of Arizona. Worse for us, the Texans have gotten up into the eastern half of the territory, and that's going to be part of Arizona, too—unless federal troops can turn 'em back."

Harry stopped and picked up a shiny pink and white seashell, dropping it into a pocket of his coat as a souvenir and totem. He took out his handkerchief and wiped his brow carefully, amazed at how hot this low country could be in what was such a cold month even in Tidewater Virginia. "And they're fixing to make this Arizona a slave state? What would it matter? There's no cotton, and no slaves that I've heard about."

"No, but if they were to build a railroad."

"A railroad to where?"

"The Pacific Ocean."

"All the way to California?"

"They wouldn't have to go that far. There's a town out there called Tuscon that lies not much more than a hundred miles from the Gulf of California."

"I've never heard of either."

"The Gulf of California's part of Mexico. Runs straight down into the Pacific Ocean. The Mexicans call it the Sea of Cortes."

"How can the Confederates build a railroad through Mexico?"

"Get the Mexicans to agree to it. Shouldn't be hard, if enough money changes hands."

Harry stopped. "How did you learn all this?"

"While you were in what Mr. Pinkerton calls 'the abodes of crime,' I was buying newspapers."

Harry shook his head, smiling. Then he took out his pocket watch and glanced at it. "We'd best be heading back."

"To the saloon or to the boat landing?"

"The latter." He paused to look at the hazy western horizon, where the sky had turned a forbidding yellow. "You know, Joseph, I expect this beach is the last safe place we're going to see for a while."

"We weren't sent here to be safe, boy."

Chapter 4

THERE was a red glow to the southeast, reflected in the clumps of cloud that hung beneath the starry sky. At first Almaden feared that Santa Fe was being burned, but as they progressed farther along the road, he realized it was merely campfires. The Confederates had arrived in Almaden's absence and taken possession of the capital. The soldiers apparently did not care that their position could be observed. They seemed to be making an advertisement of their presence—and their triumph.

"It is good you are leaving," Almaden said.

"You should come with me," said his daughter, huddled in her cloak on the wagon seat beside him.

"I cannot, Isabel. I told you why."

"We should leave the gringos to fight it out among themselves."

"Our gringos aren't doing a very good job of it."

" 'Our' gringos."

"Yes, our gringos. Abraham Lincoln's gringos."

"He is two thousand miles away. There are fires burning in Santa Fe."

"Campfires."

"Let us hope, father."

AT the next crossroads, Don Luis turned right, taking a track that veered toward the Rio Grande, and followed its valley down to the road that ran from Santa Fe to Albuquerque.

They clattered and bumped along without speaking. When Isabel was a small girl, she had often ridden with him like this, sitting close against him on a wagon seat— saying nothing, everything understood. Of all his children, she was the closest to him. They had never had a serious quarrel. Yet now he sensed the possibility of one, her silence masking anger.

At the top of the next rise, a long, low ridge giving a broad view of Santa Fe and the fires around it, Almaden halted the wagon, holding the reins wrapped tightly around his left hand while he lighted a small cigar with the other.

"Are you angry with me?" he asked, shaking out the match.

"I am angry with everything," she said. "And I am confused. I don't know now which is my country."

"Our country is Mexico."

"Yet you have become an American."

"It must be the same thing. A part of Mexico that is within the United States."

"These gringos from Texas won't tolerate that."

"They will go away. We will make them. Then President Juárez and President Lincoln will make common cause."

She brushed back some wind blown strands of her hair that had fallen across her brow. "I don't understand why you are doing this tonight."

"You think I am stealing?"

"No, I'm not saying that. Of course not. I'm sorry, father. I am very confused."

In the distance now, he could hear gunshots. They hadn't the steady sound of battle. There was no battle. Santa Fe was being occupied without interference from the Union Army. The Confederates would reign here unmolested.

The gunfire came in sporadic bursts, sounding almost in celebration, though Almaden feared it meant something worse, something in common with the pillages, rape, and murder of antiquity. He wondered who was in command of these men.

Putting his cigar between his teeth, he took up the reins, shaking them out and urging the team to lurch into motion. He felt his daughter move closer to him. He put his arm around her shoulders. She was slender, but he could feel her strength.

It was late at night when he finally arrived at the village where he had arranged a rendezvous. A small church with adjoining graveyard was at the south end of it. The inhabitants were keeping themselves indoors, and Almaden noted only the faint glow of a candle or two as they came along the main street. The moonlight had been fitful in the frequent passage of clouds, but it came forth in great brilliance as they neared the churchyard. A figure stepped from the shadows of the wall and walked into the road, leading a saddle horse. Two others were visible by the wall.

"Anselmo."

"Good evening, Don Luis."

"Not so good, this evening."

"No. Only the heavens seem happy tonight."

The man was his employee—the manager of his hacienda in the foothills of the Sangre de Cristos, with responsibilities that included his several businesses within the town as well. Almaden trusted him more than he did anyone, save Isabel.

Anselmo was a somewhat portly fellow, and as he grew older, he grew fonder of his ease, yet was no stranger to a horse. The one he rode out here was one of Almaden's best, a stallion of high temper. The animal seemed strangely calm.

"Did you have trouble?" Almaden asked.

"No, Don Luis," Anselmo replied. "But it was not easy to avoid."

"How many Rebels are in Santa Fe?"

"Only a company for now, but they are the worst people imaginable. They hardly seem soldiers. Texas roughnecks, most of them. They call themselves 'the Brigands Brigade,' and they act it. I sent the house servants to the hacienda, but that may not be far enough away. I think you should come south with us, Don Luis."

His daughter's eyes were on him, a gleam to them in the bright moonlight.

"There is nothing I would desire more," said Almaden. "But I cannot. I have no choice but to stay."

Isabel looked away, pulling her cloak close about her. The night air was turning cold.

"Is there no sign of the Union Army?" Almaden asked.

Anselmo shook his head. "A few of the New Mexico militia came in. They were with Colonel Nicolas Pinon, but I don't know where he is. They say they put up a fight down in Socorro, but surrendered when the Confederates turned artillery on them. The Confederate commander paroled them with an oath not to fight again."

The Anglo officers in the Union Army had a poor opinion of the militiamen, who were almost entirely Mexican. It distressed Almaden that his fears about his countrymen had been proven right.

"Where are Colonel Canby and Kit Carson?" he asked, referring to the principal federal commanders.

"Juan Alviso came in tonight with the militia. He says that, after Valverde, Canby and Carson holed up with the main body down at Fort Craig and sent the militia on ahead to put up a fight at Santa Fe."

"Which they did not do."

"No. Some have gone on to Fort Union."

"That's more than eighty miles away."

"Yes. Too far to send help soon."

"So it will be up to us," said Almaden.

"Us?" Anselmo had a grin one could see even if there had been no moonlight. "You are sending me away, Don Luis."

"I am sending you south with Isabel. You are to protect her with your life, but I expect you both back, and with those people from the East."

"Two gringos." Anselmo sounded sad.

"Yes. The two gringos."

"Don Luis, we have enough gringos."

*   *   *

Almaden waited until the wagon had creaked from view into the night then mounted his horse. The animal seemed pleased to have his master in the saddle and whinnied as Almaden slacked the reins to give him his head.

Gaining sight of Santa Fe once again as he followed the main highway, he took a side road that circled around the town. When he finally reentered the capital, it was from the northeast.

Confederate pickets had been placed on the outskirts of town. Not far from Fort Marcy, he encountered two men, one with a musket, the other carrying two revolvers, both dressed less in uniform than in banditos' clothes, though they were Anglos. Their beards were scruffy—grown on the trail—and they seemed churlish, perhaps because they were missing out on all the fun their compatriots appeared to be having down by the plaza.

"You halt there, you Mexican son of a bitch," said the one with the pistols.

The other thrust his musket up toward Almaden, as though it were a pike.

"I am Don Luis Almaden y Cortes. I am a member of the Santa Fe town council. I am returning to my house in the town."

"You in the New Mexico militia?"

"No. I am not military."

"What're you doing out here?"

"I took my daughter to safety, away from the fighting." The truth always made the best lie.

"There weren't no fighting. I think you're maybe a spy."

"If I were a spy, why would I ride right up to you? There are a thousand ways to sneak into this town."

The one with the pistols pondered this. The other seemed not charged with any responsibility for thought.

Almaden always kept cigars and a small bottle of tequila in his saddlebags.

"Allow me to present you with a welcoming gift from the people of Santa Fe," he said.

The two raised their weapons higher. Moving slowly, he pulled out the bottle and tossed it to the man with the pistols, who caught it clumsily.

"It will warm you," Almaden said, urging his horse forward. "It will be a cold night."

They let him pass.

TROTTING down the Paseo de Peralta, Almaden began to wish the two pickets had been successful in turning him away. Though only a company of Texans was occupying Santa Fe, there seemed to be drunken men on every corner and in every doorway. They had forced the entrances of numerous houses, and there was looting. Most of it was just for food and drink, but they were hauling out valuables as well, especially from the more expensive residences. They were taking women, too. A girl Almaden recognized as the daughter of a friend was being dragged, crying and cursing, into a courtyard.

Almaden halted and turned his horse. Before he could say a word, one of the men dropped the girl's arm and pulled out a revolver. He was very drunk. It would affect his aim but not his intent. Almaden had much yet to do.

"If you harm her, someone in this town will kill you," he said, speaking quietly but firmly.

"You get out of here now, or I will kill you, sir."

"Her father is a friend to your Confederacy," Almaden said. "You will have to answer to your commander."

The man, unsteady on his feet, let go the girl then fired a shot in the air. The girl screamed, and ran off.

"Git!" said the man, to Almaden.

Almaden put heels to flanks, and his horse moved quickly to a trot. He hadn't far to go.

The door to his house stood open. One of the soldiers appeared in it as Almaden came up. The fellow clutched a bottle of wine in one hand and a silver crucifix in the other. It had belonged to Almaden's mother and had been hanging on the wall above the bed on which she had died.

He could take no more. He leapt from the saddle and fell upon the man, ripping the crucifix from his hand. The soldiers staggered back and pulled out a long Bowie knife. It was a mean-looking weapon, but too heavy and unwieldy to be effective in such tight quarters—at least against a sober adversary.

Almaden feinted to one side, then whacked at the man's knife arm with the crucifix, hitting bone and knocking the weapon to the ground. Stepping back, he kicked the wretch as forcefully as he could and the villain went down, crying out. Almaden kicked him one more time, but by then a seemingly unending stream of Texans came pouring forth from his house, one of them gripping his arms from behind. Another began hitting him—chest and belly. Then yet another pushed forward and struck him on the side of the head with a pistol butt.

He sank to his knees, his battle ended—and lost.

Chapter 5

HARRY and Leahy had taken a stagecoach to San Antonio over the worst road Harry had traveled since he had last passed through Virginia's well-named Dismal Swamp. From there, they'd traveled to El Paso in a crudely built conveyance that was the least comfortable he'd ever set backside in, traveling over what amounted to no road at all. Their driver simply followed the tracks and hardened ruts of other vehicles that had passed this way before them—their passage a wander across a scrubby, dun-colored and utterly featureless wasteland.

It was an amazement that the United States had actually waged a bloody war to acquire this place and was bent on doing so again.

"California was always the prize," Leahy said. "They say it's the land of milk and honey."

"And New Mexico?"

"The savages like it there," said the man seated opposite, a preacher in worn black clothes, who appeared unhappy with his destination.

"Savages?" Harry asked.

"Indians. The primitive heathen—a people rightly fit for so God-forsaken a land."

"How savage are these savages?" Leahy asked.

The preacher took another swig of the whiskey that was being passed around the coach, then wiped his mouth on the back of his hand. "Killed my fellow pastor. The Reverend Stoakes and his wife. Kiowas, they were. Cut 'em up horrible."

"This was in El Paso?" Harry asked.

The preacher shook his head, sadly. "Was a raiding party came south and east of there. Hit the stagecoach stop where they had halted. Massacred everyone. Taking advantage of the current unpleasantness, the Kiowas were."

"Most of the Indians in these parts are on our side," said one of the officers, after taking his turn at the bottle.

"Those Kiowas weren't. Only their own side. They'd take your hair as quick as a Yankee's."

Harry bent forward to look out the window. The landscape was so desolate, they might as well have been on the moon.

His two Navy Colt revolvers, small Derringer, and the sheath knife in his boot had seemed a formidable arsenal in Washington City. Here, he felt almost unarmed.

Squinting against the dust, he saw ahead a long, low ridge, but no buildings, no landmarks, no humans.

"Do you suppose the driver knows where he's going?" Harry said to Leahy. "We seem to weave instead of following a straight course."

"Sure he does, laddy buck. It's his skin as well as ours."

They were jounced high in their seats when the left rear struck a mound or rock. The sixth passenger aboard—a well-dressed, middle-aged man who had been dozing—awakened and joined the conversation for the first time in miles.

"He knows the way, depend upon it," the man said. "We lurch from watering hole to watering hole, stagecoach stop to stagecoach stop. Miss the mark and we all die."

"Has that happened?" Harry asked.

"Out here, everything happens," said the man. "It's different where I'm going."

The others sat and waited for him to speak further, but he did not.

"And where is that?" Leahy asked, finally.

"North of El Paso. Up in the Colorado Territory. There's a place sweet with water. Trees and green valleys. And gold and silver."

"And Federal soldiers," said one of the Rebel officers. "Why go there?"

"Time I get there, maybe they'll be gone."

Gold and silver. It occurred to Harry there was more to worry one here than Kiowa Indians.

LUIS Almaden had been thrown into the Santa Fe jail, sharing a large, crowded common cell with an assortment of drunks, criminals, and Mexicans and Anglos suspected of being Union sympathizers. Almaden knew a number of his fellow prisoners and was surprised at how accurate the assessment of the loyalty of these men had been.

Perhaps the Confederates had had help in making this identification.

He had made a place for himself in a rear corner, calculating that he'd be at some distance from his jailors and any mischief they might have in mind. His head, arms, and chest still hurt, but he managed to make himself comfortable propping himself against the wall and stretching out his legs.

The food they'd given him was vile—a greasy stew of bread, weeds, and strands of some strange meat. When the guard opened the cell door on the second morning of his confinement, Almaden feared it was to serve breakfast. Instead, the man stepped into the room, searched the faces before him, and finally set eyes on Almaden in his corner.

"You, come," he commanded.

Almaden waited, wondering if the soldiers ransacking his house might have found something incriminating—or whether one of his friends had talked about him to the new authorities.

Closing his eyes, Almaden pretended not to have noticed the summons, but it did no good. The soldier waded through the cell's other inmates and leaned down to grab Almaden's shoulder.

"Get up, damn it! Somebody wants to see you!"

Almaden got to his feet without assistance, an assortment of pains afflicting him in the process.

"What is it you want?" Almaden asked, with as much politeness as he could muster in the circumstance.

"Follow me."

As though fearful they might be invited to join him, the others in the cell shrank back. The door clanked shut and then was locked behind him.

"You're a free man," the guard said.

THE sunlight out in the street was harshly bright, and Almaden's eyes required considerable adjusting. Stepping away from the jail's gate, he put up his hand as a shield against the glare, taking note of a black barouche with a matched pair of bay horses in harness. In it sat two women—one plain and brown and very Mexican; the other tall, fair-skinned, dark-haired, and striking.

As always, she wore black. Her gaze was steady and fixed on him, but she made no sign of greeting.

The soldier who had accompanied Almaden outside shoved him forward.

"Come along," he said. "Move. Get in the carriage."

He held the door open as Almaden climbed aboard, taking a rearward-facing seat.

"Good morning, Mercedes," Almaden said. "This is very unexpected."

"I was very unhappy to hear that you had been detained, Don Luis. I simply could not imagine how they could have made such a mistake."

She produced a fan from her lap and set it to fluttering before her face, though this early in the morning the air was quite cool.

"It was no mistake, senora. Your 'Southern gentlemen' were looting my house. I tried to stop them, and so they decided I was their enemy."

The fan increased its fluttering, then stopped.

"N'importe. Santa Fe was held by the enemy, Don Luis. Such things happen in war."

The driver turned the carriage around in the street, bumping a wheel into a rut. Jostled, Almaden winced with the pain it caused then tried to erase all signs of his discomfort.

"There was no fight for this town, Mercedes," he said. "They just came in and started pillaging—starting with the wealthiest households. I am surprised your house was not gone over."

"It was not, sir. It flies the Stars and Bars."

Of course.

"Is it to your house you're taking me?" he said. "Or to mine?"

He sensed her smiling behind her fan.

"To neither—yet. We are going to the Palace of the Governors, where I am going to introduce you to a gentleman it would do you well to know. Major Charles Pyron. He commands the battalion that has occupied Santa Fe. I have told him you might be of service to him."

"That's why I was let out of that jail?"

"It is, Luis."

"Then you should turn around and take me back there."

She leaned forward, placing a hand on his knee. Blanca, the brown-faced woman next to her, paid no attention. As Mercedes's maid, she had been witness to many such intimacies.

"Luis," said Mercedes. "Don't talk that way, I beg you. Major Pyron has restored order here, but they are dealing severely with Union sympathizers. You are on the town council, and you attacked Confederate soldiers. Continue in his reckless manner, and you could be shot."

She was not exaggerating.

Mercedes sat back, confident that she had persuaded him. Almaden thought upon the matter—not for very long.

"How is it I am to serve him? If he is going to ask me to identify Union men—well, Mercedes, that is something I would never do."

"I know that. As I know you. But I do not know what

he will ask you. I would urge you to be circumspect and try to be helpful if you can. They have swept all before them, Luis. They hope to go on to Colorado—and to California. They rule here now. You must accommodate yourself to them, as you did when the United States took over this territory."

He looked along the street. There were soldiers everywhere, but they were standing or moving about in orderly fashion.

"Why do you say 'them?' " he asked. "Why not 'we?' "

"I am overjoyed by the wonderful turn of events, Luis. But I worry about some of my friends. And I especially worry about you." Her smile was very sweet. "Perhaps we should have cleaned you up first. You are still the handsomest man in New Mexico, but you look as disreputable as one of those 'Brigands.' "

PYRON had taken over an office in the Palace of Governors with a door opening onto the long central courtyard of the building. There were two soldiers standing just outside it.

The major sat behind his desk, feeling and looking irritable. He rose as Mercedes entered, but pointedly ignored Almaden. When everyone was seated again, he at last turned to look at his prisoner.

"You were with the militia? You were one of Pinon's men who was paroled?"

"No, senor," said Almaden. "I am on the town council, but I have not served in the military. Not in this war."

"You were in the Mexican thing?"

"I am Mexican. I fought the invaders."

Pyron was studying him carefully. "We're the invaders now."

Almaden hesitated. "I would hope you are liberators."

The major grinned. "We didn't come into New Mexico just to pass through, Mister."

"So I presumed."

Pyron abruptly got to his feet, going to a wall, where a large paper map had been nailed up. "Come here, please, Senor Almaden."

Don Luis did as bidden. The map showed all of New Mexico Territory and portions of Colorado and the Republic of Mexico.

Pyron's finger went to the southern end of the Sangre de Cristo Mountains. "This pass here . . ."

"Glorieta," said Almaden.

"Yes, Glorieta. Is this the only way around the mountains? There's not another pass closer to Fort Union? Another way for them to come at us?"

Almaden had to make a quick decision. "No, senor. Nothing near. They would have to go north and go over the mountains up around Taos. Or else south to Santa Rosa. There's no other road."

"I don't care about roads. No other track? No trail?"

"Animal trails. Indian trails. But nothing near. Nothing useful."

"So if we stop 'em in that pass, they're stopped?"

"*Sí*, senor."

Pyron stared at the map. "Madame Beignet says you can be trusted. That you don't like the Yankees."

"I am an honorable man, Major. And, I fought them in the last war."

Pyron gave him a sharp look. "Fought us, Mister Almaden." He jabbed at the map. "You're absolutely sure this is the only way in?"

"There is a road north from Pecos that follows a stream up into the mountains—nearly to the top. There's a little village there, called Holy Ghost. But they'd be a long time getting up there and then a long time coming down the other side of the range. Very rough country. Very steep. No place for an army. No sir."

Pyron rubbed his chin then turned away from the map for good. He remained standing, an indication the audience was over. "Thank you. And thank you, Madame Beignet."

"When you go into that canyon," Almaden said. "I will go with you. I will show you the route—what is possible, what is not."

Mercedes smiled. "You can trust Don Luis, Major. Just as I told you."

Chapter 6

Harry stood at the rail of the El Paso horse dealer's mostly empty corral, looking at four of the most pathetic specimens he had ever encountered in the six years he'd been practicing the livestock trade. One animal was obviously lame. Another was blind in one eye. The third shook convulsively, and the fourth was woefully underfed and bore so many whip marks he looked half zebra. He wondered why they hadn't been sold for meat.

"This is all you have?" he asked the proprietor, a scrawny geezer who much resembled his wares.

Harry had been hoping to find at least an approximation of his big horse Rocket, whom he had sent to his farm near Shepherdstown, Virginia, for safekeeping from federal equine press gangs. Rocket was a very large animal, and not much in a race. But he was as dependable as sunrise and strong enough to take even this wild country in stride.

"Sure is all I got—and you're lucky to be finding any. Before they pulled out, General Sibley's army commandeered pretty much every spare mount between here and Fort Bliss."

"And they left these fine animals?"

"Someone'll buy 'em. Maybe you, if you're tired of walkin'."

The proprietor was an old man, with a bush of a beard and patched clothing. Harry supposed he'd made more than enough money to richly improve his appearance if he chose to and that his shabbiness was a device to persuade customers of his honesty. Harry was not persuaded.

"I am indeed tired of shank's mare," Harry said. "But I've a long way to go, and riding one of these could get me killed. Drop dead on me in the middle of the desert."

"On foot, you won't even get into the desert."

Harry lighted one of his small cigars, offering one to the dealer. "I won't argue with you about that. But surely, sir, there are better mounts to be had somewhere."

"Am I the first place you looked?"

"No. The fourth."

"Thought so. Four of us is all there is. Only other place you're going to find horseflesh is in Mexico. Unless you want to wait."

"Wait for what?"

"Pretty soon, Mexico's going to be part of the Confederate States. Leastwise part of it is."

"How can that be? The Confederacy's having a hell of a time just hanging on to what it's already got."

"Maybe so, but I heard it from an officer who bought my two best horses. Mexican government's going to sell Chihuahua, Sonora, and Lower California to Jeff Davis. That's what he said."

"Why would the Mexican government do that? They fought a war to keep the half of their country we took."

"We?"

"We Americans."

"Well, sir. It's no exaggeration, I do believe, to say that times have changed."

"Yes, I'm afraid you're right."

"Afraid?"

"I'm not fond of war."

"Well, I ain't either, except it stands to make me a pile of money."

"I'm not going to pay you a pile of money for any of these poor devils."

"Then I guess you won't be buyin' any."

Harry sighed, tossing down the remnants of his little cigar. "I'll take the one-eyed one." He studied the other three, one by one. "And the skinny one."

"A hundred dollars."

"Each?"

"Both."

"Very well." He dug out the gold coins necessary. "That will, of course, include bridles and saddles."

The man simply stared at him.

"I'm going into New Mexico after horses," Harry said. "I may have to take them off the Yankees, but if I find some, I'm bringing them back here. For sale. Shall it be to you?"

"I pay top dollar."

"I'm sure you do," Harry said, with a doubtful grin. "But I'm not buying these without tack. And not a penny more than your outrageous price."

The man made a face, his contortion twisting his beard oddly, then he gave a nod.

"Normal times, they wouldn't be worth so much."

"Normal times, you'd be in jail for highway robbery."

THE saddles the man provided looked as worn and tattered as the animals. Harry checked the girth on the one-eyed mount, deciding he'd better avoid any fast turns. Looking over the creature, it occurred to him that "fast" was probably an inappropriate term.

Going around to the side with the good eye, he stroked the animal's nose a moment, then climbed into the saddle, feeling it slip slightly. He reached to take the reins of the skinny horse that stood beside his.

"You find anything out there," said the dealer. "I'll pay you twenty a head."

"If I find anything out there," Harry said, "we'll talk about it."

He started out of the stable yard.

"You sure you're a horse trader?" said the other. "Never knew one dress so good as you."

"I'm an honest man," Harry said.

"Never knew one of those neither."

LEAHY stood and stared in disbelief at the animal Harry had brought him, then walked around it slowly.

"I don't share your skill at riding these animals, laddy buck," said Leahy. "But I am by far your superior at picking them."

"You may not believe me, but these are probably the finest animals for sale in El Paso."

"I do believe you, boyo. So let us absent ourselves from El Paso pronto."

"Pronto?"

"It means quick, or soon."

"Pronto it is, then."

THE thumping at the front door awakened Almaden instantly, though Mercedes remained asleep. He looked down upon her, recalling with some savor the happiness of the night, then eased himself from beneath the counterpane and off the bed.

He went to the window. There were three horses and two Confederate soldiers outside in the street. The missing man, he presumed, was in the doorway just below, responsible for all the noise.

"What are you doing?" asked Mercedes, awake now.

"Someone's at your door."

"There is always someone at my door. Come back to bed."

Almaden started to pull on his clothes. "They are Rebel soldiers."

"Undoubtedly drunk. They come around all the time. Please, Luis."

"They do not appear to be drunk."

She swore—in French, then threw back the covers and went to the chair where she had left her robe. "I'll go down. You come with me. Do you have a gun?"

"No," he said.

Swearing once more, she went to her dresser and opened the top drawer, removing a long-barreled revolver. "Let's go."

*　*　*

THE man at the door was in no way drunk. The emphatic manner in which he'd been rapping had to do with a mixture of urgency and frustration that had also contorted his features. "You've got to come to Major Pyron's right away," he said to Almaden.

"Why? What's happened?"

"I don't know what's happened, but whatever it is, it's got the major powerful wakeful this hour of the night."

"He's at the Palace of the Governors?"

"No. He's at this house he commandeered. You're to come with me."

PYRON was seated on a horsehair sofa in the parlor of the house, still in uniform but with his coat unbuttoned and his boots off. There was a whiskey bottle on the table in front of him and a cup in his hand. Two aides were in the room with him, a captain in a rough-looking mismatch of a uniform and a sleepy sergeant.

"What have I done now?" asked Almaden.

"You have done nothing, Don Luis, but there is something I would like you to do." Pyron eased back and propped his stockinged feet upon the table.

Almaden waited. Pyron gestured for him to sit down on a wooden chair opposite. He did so.

"The Yankees have moved out of Fort Union and are heading this way," Pyron resumed. "Just had a dispatch rider come in with the news. I mean to move out at dawn and meet 'em. I want you to come along."

Almaden thought upon this. With Anselmo, Isabel, and his two sons gone, he had no one truly reliable to look after

his properties and interests in Santa Fe. There was Mercedes, but her reliability was still an open question.

"Why would you need me?"

"I want you to guide us through that canyon."

"I would be glad to help you in any way, but why do
you need a guide? Did not your dispatch rider just come
through there?"

"Yes he did. And he got lost twice on the way. There
are a lot of nooks and crannies up there, and I want to
learn about every inch of them. From you. And I want to
see if maybe there isn't another way after all to get to Santa
Fe besides that pass."

If Pyron's force ran head on into the Federals, they'd be
stopped cold. They might even get themselves ambushed,
if word of their march could somehow be gotten to the
Union men.

"There isn't another way," said Almaden. "I told you."

"I want you to show me for certain. I want you to find
me some good ambush ground. You were in the military,
weren't you?"

Almaden smiled, he hoped not too wickedly. "Yes. But
on the other side. The Mexican Army."

"Fighting U.S. government troops?"

"Yes. Mostly Texans."

Pyron let that pass. "You were born here. Grew up
here?"

"Yes."

"Madame Beignet vouches for you a hundred percent,
Don Luis. I want you with me. We're forming up at the
plaza in three hours."

"Very well. As you wish."

"Your new government will be grateful."

Chapter 7

To his surprise, Harry found the one-eyed horse to be an uncomplaining and steadfast mount. They were a day out of Las Cruces, on the hard trail north to Santa Fe, and the animal had yet to nip, complain, falter, or evidence any other sign of weakness or disagreeableness. It had a way of keeping its head turned to the right for a fuller view of the way ahead, but that was a small annoyance. Under the circumstances, Harry had to consider the horse a bargain. He'd seen worse mounts ridden into battle by officers of both armies in the East.

Nothing so salubrious could be said for Leahy's sickly nag, which could manage only a sort of plod and seemed shortly bound to join the poor creatures whose bleached bones were scattered here and there along the way.

They were keeping to the east bank of the Rio Grande and had passed through a number of towns and villages. None of them, including Las Cruces, possessed horses for sale or rent.

"If we don't find one for sale pretty soon, boyo, we're

going to have to steal me a better beast," Leahy said, as they broke camp for another long day in the saddle.

The Irishman had given up his black derby for a broad-brimmed hat more suitable to the climate and had acquired a sheepskin coat, but he'd retained his too-tight black suit. He was an excellent intelligence agent, but a poor horseman, putting Harry in mind of Cervantes's Quixote. He could only wonder why Pinkerton had sent either of them west. Perhaps the Secret Service chief really did want them out of the Eastern theater of the war and cared little what fate they might meet out here.

"I'm told they hang you without the nicety of a trial out here for doing that," Harry said.

"That gloomy prospect dogs us for a number of reasons."

"Yes, but why hasten it?"

"Laddy, I am bloody well not going to walk to Santa Fe."

"If it comes to it, Joseph, you can take mine and I'll walk."

"No you don't. Mr. Pinkerton said both of us, and it's both of us who will be riding into Santa Fe."

How Leahy proposed to achieve this miracle, he did not say. But if he was counting on divine intervention, something of the sort was actually what occurred. In late morning, with the climbing sun warming the desert air, they saw a horse off to the east, standing perfectly still, but with its head lowered.

Harry was wearing his spectacles and could see that it was an animal in very good condition—a sand-colored horse, well configured, with a white mane and long, flowing tail of the same color.

"Perhaps his owner is nearby," Harry said, heading One-Eye over to investigate. Leahy followed, taking out a long-barreled revolver and resting it on his saddle pommel—as Harry neglected to do.

There was a reason the animal hadn't budged. Its rider lay face up at the horse's feet, staring up at the desert sky, the reins still wound around his left hand. The man's once-white shirt bore a glistening swath of blood that extended into the cloth of his expensive black coat, and there were splotches of it on the horse's saddle as well.

Leahy dismounted and knelt beside the fallen horseman, placing his fingers at the side of the man's neck. Frowning, he sat back on his heels.

"What's wrong?" Harry asked. It was a stupid question. What was wrong was that they had a corpse on their hands. He knelt close. "Has he been dead long?"

"He's still alive," said Leahy. "An amazement. Been shot through the back." He laid a finger on the man's chest. "This here's the exit wound."

"Can we help him?"

Leahy gave him a doubtful glance.

He had been a police detective in Boston before joining Allan Pinkerton's Secret Service and was a skilled and efficient searcher. As gently as possible, he began going through the man's pockets, removing a wallet, several papers, and a pocket watch.

"This is villainy, Joseph," Harry said. "Robbing the dead."

"As I said, that is not yet the case. I want to find out who he is."

Leahy settled into a cross-legged position that Harry, twelve years the Irishman's junior, would have found uncomfortable and began examining the man's papers. Harry came near and freed the horse's reins from the stricken man's grip, pulling the animal aside. A stallion, it was altogether magnificent. It was remarkable that he was still standing here at liberty.

The saddle was Spanish, made of fine-quality leather, with a burnished metal trim. After a moment's hesitation, Harry loosed the fastenings of the saddlebags, finding within the first one some clothing, a razor and tooth-cleaning brush wrapped in a towel, and a small bottle of tequila. Reaching into the other, he found a large, heavy, leather bag, tied with a thong. He pulled it out and opened it.

"Well, now," he said. "This makes matters interesting."

Leahy said nothing.

Harry gave the bag a vigorous, clinking shake. "There's gold in here. Gold coins."

Leahy did not look up.

Harry shook the bag again—twice. "Gold, Joseph. Must be a thousand dollars."

The Irishman got back to his feet, his eyes still hard on the letter he was holding. "This is about the Rebels." He crinkled his brow, peering closer. "It says they're about to take Santa Fe, the bastards."

"Was there a battle?"

"Doesn't say." He handed the letter to Harry, then knelt beside the injured man again.

"It's addressed to a Don Luis Almaden y Cortes. Do you suppose this is him?"

"Ask him."

Harry leaned close to the man's face. "Are you Don Luis Almaden?"

The injured one's eyes fixed on Harry's, as though seeing him for the first time.

"San Jeronimo," he said, his voice a barely audible croak of a moan.

"He says his name is San Jeronimo."

"There's another letter. My Spanish isn't good, but I know Portuguese, and it's close."

"Where did you learn Portuguese?"

"From the fishermen in Massachusetts. This letter says there was another battle. A Rebel general named Sibley defeated a Federal force under a Colonel Canby at a town north of here called Valverde. Canby retreated to a Fort Craig, and Sibley has passed him by, heading for Santa Fe."

He read further. "Like the man said in the stagecoach. They're fixing to sweep all the way into Colorado territory. Probably seize and hold the gold and silver mines there. All that stands in their way is a Federal force up at Fort Union."

"Perhaps Mister San Jeronimo can tell us something," Harry said, nodding to the wounded man.

Leahy looked. "No. I think now he's dead." He leaned close. "Yes. *Muerto*, as he would say."

"Poor fellow. I wonder who shot him."

"In this country, could have been anyone."

Leahy went through the man's pockets again, finding nothing of consequence. He stood up, wiping his brow, though there was not so much heat. "He's a well-dressed Mexican, sure enough. A gentleman. Maybe an aristocrat."

"Maybe he is the Don Luis the letter's addressed to." Harry lifted the gold. "This is a lot of money for a lone rider to be carrying in country like this."

"Unless he took it from someone else," said Leahy.

"And that someone shot him in the back."

Leahy's eyes went to the low mountains to the north. "And maybe is looking for him now."

"Then we should be leaving this place."

They both looked to the sand-colored horse.

"You covet that animal, don't you, Harry?"

"How biblical of you, Joseph. I do indeed. That horse is as possessed of every good quality as my own Rocket— and I think must have even greater speed. But, you take him, sir. I'm content with this half-sighted fellow."

Leahy grinned. "He'd be recognized, this handsome one. Might bring trouble. Maybe it would be better if he went with me."

"With you? What do you mean? Where are you going?"

"Someone has to get this letter to the Federals. They've got to be warned."

Harry got out the map he had purchased in El Paso. It was sketchy, but the places mentioned in the two letters were on it. "There's a Fort Union east of Santa Fe, on the other side of the mountains. There'd be Union troops there, I think."

"Then that's where I'll go."

"You mean to cut across country?"

"Fastest way."

"We can both go."

"We have our duty to Mr. Pinkerton, Captain Raines. Let's not be shirkers. The order was to find the Confederate forces here and divine their intentions."

Harry went to Leahy and snatched the letter from his hand, waving it in the air. "We've found the Rebels. They're in Santa Fe, or about to be. And we've divined their intentions. They're bound for Colorado and gold."

Leahy shook his head, wearily. "One of us must go to Fort Union—in the utmost haste. The other of us must follow the river north until the Confederate army is encountered. And meet with our agent in Santa Fe. He will have much to tell us." He took the letter back. "More than we find in this."

Harry shrugged, accepting the obvious. "I suppose you are right."

"Not always. But surely I am right about this." He pocketed the letter, then paused. "It needn't be me who rides for Fort Union. You could go—on this horse you favor so much. I'll proceed to Santa Fe. I hear it's pleasant there."

Harry kicked at the dust, then looked again at his map, finding Las Cruces and then following the line of the river north. Then he faced to the east, where a jagged purple line of mountains rose against the cloudless sky.

"Those must be the San Andres range," he said.

Leahy came to his side, squinting at the map. "Aye."

"Whichever of us goes to Fort Union will have to get to the other side of it."

"There's a pass or draw back up the road a bit," Leahy said, noting it on the map. "Here. Northeast of Las Cruces."

"Not much water on the other side of those mountains. It would be a hard ride. You're a city man, Joseph. Do you think you can manage?"

"Harry, I went through the famine in Ireland. There's not much in the way of hardship I don't know."

"The other one of us would have to continue along the river alone," Harry said. "The trail curves to the west, away from the mountains—up through this valley." He leaned closer to read aloud the words on the map. " 'Jornada del Muerto.' "

Leahy grinned. "It means 'Dead Man's Journey.' "

"Fine thing to name a road."

"Fine thing to name anything around here that claims to be a road."

Whichever way he chose to go, Harry would have to complete his journey alone—in the strangest country he had ever seen, a place so bewilderingly wild and empty as to be scarcely imagined.

"Very well, Joseph. You go to Fort Union. I'll go to Santa Fe. On the horse I've got. How shall we ever meet again?"

"That'll be decided by the fortunes of war, I'd say." He began to loosen the sand-colored horse's cinch.

"What are you doing?" Harry asked. "That's a fine saddle. Cost a lot."

"And will be recognized for that very reason," Leahy said, pulling it off as though effortlessly and setting it on the ground. "I'll put the wretched one I have been riding on in its place."

The dead man appeared to be looking on, evidencing neither opprobrium nor approval.

"What are we to do with the gentleman?" Harry asked.

Leahy contemplated their surroundings. "There are rocks in those gullies by the river. We don't have time to dig a hole for him, but we can cover him up a bit. If someone comes along and investigates the cairn, maybe they'll give him a decent burial."

"Do you expect you'll find anyone that charitable in this country?"

"As I think upon it, no. But I don't want to tarry."

ALMADEN rode beside Major Pyron into the narrowness of the gorge, a lieutenant and a color sergeant trailing just behind. Stretching back to the beginning of this part of Glorieta Pass, threading through what was called Apache Canyon, Pyron's small army of about four hundred men followed, most of them mounted and in column. The main Confederate body, led by a General Sibley, was still far to the south, coming on slow.

After another two miles, the trail would rise as it climbed to the summit of the pass, descending on the other side through a long defile that led to the Pecos River and the campground at Kozlowski's Ranch. In all, Glorieta was a trek of twelve miles—the threat of ambush at every turning.

There was a high mesa to the right and the southern tip of the Sangre de Cristo range on the left. Halfway through the pass, they would come to Pigeon's Ranch—called that because the owner, a Frenchman named Alexander Valle, danced the fandango at local fiestas just like a pigeon. Almaden guessed Pyron would push on rather than camp there.

Pyron wanted more than to defeat whatever Federals he encountered along this road. He had brought all his supplies, carried in wagons he'd left at the entrance to Apache Canyon. Once he was through the pass, presuming he hadn't encountered the Union army, he'd send a rider back with orders for the wagons to join him. He'd wait at the campground for the rest of the Rebels to come up, then push on with their long planned invasion of Colorado. There'd be no supply line. The Rebels would have to live off these wagons—and the surrounding country—much as General Winfield Scott had done in the war with Mexico, marching from Vera Cruz to Mexico City. Every Mexican had reason to rue that long ago gamble, as they might this one now.

Unless the Confederates could be stopped in the pass.

Pyron was an imaginative, intelligent, quick, and decisive leader. Almaden had not met the man's superior, General Sibley, but had heard that he was overly fond of whiskey and inattentive to all else if he was denied it, or too well supplied with it. The general had invented a large camp tent that had become popular with both Northern and Southern armies. Otherwise, his service was mostly a boon to the North. The Confederate cause here in the canyon benefited from his decision to stay behind.

Pyron had sent a scouting party of some thirty riders ahead of the main column. Their dust was still hanging in the air. Close behind this advance guard was a rolling battery of two six-pounder field guns surrounded by a company of mounted Texans carrying their Lone Star flag instead of the Confederate "Stars and Bars."

They'd been yipping and rowdying a bit on the road out of Santa Fe but had settled down and quieted once in the canyon, knowing a fusilade of musket balls might greet them at any point.

"Not a sign of the Yankees," said Pyron, eyeing the canyon rims to either side.

"They may be cautious."

"What's on the other side of the pass?"

"Kozlowski's Ranch."

"Kozlowski?"

"Man from Poland. Martin Kozlowski. He has some of the finest land to be found in this part of New Mexico. Well watered. Many trees. Rich pastures. There's a campground nearby, favored by the wagon trains."

"They might be there, the Yankees?" Pyron asked.

"If they wished to camp, they would be drawn to it."

"If we get to other end before they do, we've got 'em, right? They'll have to attack. We can find good defensive positions."

"The high ground is full of them," Almaden said.

"We should hurry the pace."

"We should be cautious. This is the most dangerous ground to fight a war on in New Mexico." It seemed to please the major to hear Almaden say "we," as though his utterance of that simple word reaffirmed the faith Pyron had placed in him.

The major's attention went to a rock-strewn hill just ahead and to their right. Its boulders provided cover enough for a company of sharpshooters. Almaden wondered how well the Union commanders knew this ground. They would have Mexicans like himself with them—members of the New Mexico militia. If all had gone well, one if not both of his sons were likely among them.

They might be around the next bend. Almaden could all but hear the sudden explosion of rifle and musket fire, see the falling bodies on both sides. What irony if he and his boys should be among the first casualties. Above all things, someone had written, fear irony.

His horse whinnied and tossed its head, side-stepping to the right. He pulled back on the reins, just enough to assert his control, then let them fall slack, giving the stallion his head.

Pyron took note of this. "He's nervous," he said.

"Unused to armies," Almaden said.

"After we deal with these Yankees, you'll be free to go home. Or are you familiar with the trails in Colorado?"

"No, I am not," said Almaden, lying. "But the way to Denver is plain. You follow the eastern slope of the mountains straight up to it."

Pyron squinted ahead, to fresh dust kicked up by his scouts. "We'd be smart just to hold on to this pass. A strong force in here could hold off anything the federal government has in the West."

"You do not need me to tell you that," Almaden said—smiling, to show that this was not complaint.

"No. But you can help." The major sighed. "I need to know where to choose my ground."

"Do you want me to ride on ahead?"

A grin. "Can't talk to you that way."

"As you wish. I am at your service."

"So it seems. I took you along on Madame Beignet's word about you. Glad to see you're proving her right. Don't know why so many of you people have thrown in with the other side."

Almaden kept tight control of his expression. "My people have many opinions. Some are with the Union. Some side with you. Most wish you'd both go away."

"That include you?"

"I wish you'd get your war over so I can resume living my life in peace. That's why I'm here. To help you get it over."

"You've no opinion on the slavery question?"

Almaden shook his head. "I've no slaves. There is little need or use for them in New Mexico."

"Madame Beignet has slaves."

"Two. Her maid and her cook, whom she brought from New Orleans. Her other servants are local people—paid wages."

"But she believes in our cause?"

"Oh yes. She is incurably romantic. She thinks of you as the chivalry of old."

Pyron smiled. "You two are very good friends?"

Almaden looked to the trail ahead, where a log bridge crossed a dry arroyo perhaps fifteen feet across. "Yes. Old friends."

*   *   *

THE first report had a sharp, ringing echo to it, sounding like a stone thrown hard against a large rock. Then two more such claps quickly followed, and all at once there was a fury of them.

Pyron stood up in his stirrups, as his sergeant rode up fast.

"Have them unlimber the guns!" Pyron said. He looked quickly to Almaden. "No way around this canyon? You're sure? Damned sure?"

Almaden shook his head.

Pyron spurred his horse. Almaden followed, but steered his stallion obliquely off to the right, into the rocks and scrubby brush to the side.

HARRY watched Leahy's tall, straight figure diminish into the east. He waited, sitting uneasily in his own saddle, for several minutes, as though expecting the Irishman to change his mind and come back.

He was not only losing a friend—perhaps for a few days or weeks, perhaps forever—but his only contact with the East. The magnitude of his homesickness was now as great as this vast Western wilderness. There was no place on the continent Harry knew of as lushly green as his native Virginia. Here, that color seemed alien. The East was a place of cities. Even muddy, fetid, ramshackle Washington City was turning into a sophisticated metropolis, as it swelled with hordes of new people and the works of war. In New Mexico, "metropolis" was a pointless word. Galveston and El Paso back down in Texas were really no more than rude villages.

In the East, in a perverse way, the war made sense—

two nations desperately fighting for their survival. There was room in these empty Western wastes for many nations. Millions of settlers would have to move here before there was the wherewithal for a quarrel on the scale of that being waged in the mountains, forests, meadows, and farm fields between the Federal City and Richmond.

Leahy had now vanished. Harry's eyes lifted to the crooked line of the horizon. He tried to imagine the immensity of territory that separated him from the familiar world of the Willard Hotel, Pennsylvania Avenue, and the huge national Capitol, with its new dome arising.

The distance separated him from the two women he held most dear, both beautiful, both actresses. One was the English-born Caitlin Howard, who despised the institution of slavery. The other, Louise Devereux, was from New Orleans, working for the South in the same dark line of work as he. Caitlin had left him long ago for an actor named John Wilkes Booth. Louise, he had said farewell to in Richmond several weeks before, uncertain as to her feelings for him, and her loyalties to the national flag, though she had shared his bed.

There was a thought to warm him.

He patted One-Eye on the neck. He had one friend left out here. With a gentle slap of rein, he turned the horse back onto the trail to the north.

THE rest of Pyron's troops were going forward at a rush, on horseback and on foot. Ahead, Almaden could see gunsmoke rising above the small hill that marked the next turn in the trail. He kept his horse edging to the side, obliquely climbing the slope of the ridge to the right. Finally, near the top, he dismounted. Taking revolver in hand, he moved forward, keeping pace with the progress of Pyron's men below.

There were a few of the Rebel skirmishers moving along the slope with him, but not enough, if they wished to win the day. What Pyron needed was to get two or three companies of troops over the top of the hill ahead, taking high ground above the Union force's left flank. Maybe he would come to see that.

Without much aim, Almaden let loose a shot in that direction as a sign of his participation and fidelity. When he finally reached that dusty summit, with two Confederates a few feet behind him, he crouched low, moving to the side of a high, cracked boulder, as a Union bullet sang through the air above him.

"You're gonna get that fine horse of yours kilt, amigo," said one of the Rebels—like the others, a Texan.

"May need him," said Almaden. He smiled, ducking as another round came his way.

There were more boulders and some juniper pine off to the right, where the ridge began to climb again. Below, through the smoke and hanging dust, he could see Pyron's men fanning out to either side of the trail. The Union troops were quite near—trying to keep to cover. The noise was overwhelming, swelled by continuous echoing off the canyon slopes and rocky walls.

Almaden's horse pulled his reins free and nervously edged away. Keeping to his rock, Almaden did not try to recapture the animal, hoping he'd find shelter on his own.

Pyron was down by his two field pieces, which were being quickly brought to bear. The Union force had massed in a thick front across the road, but the formation began to pull apart as the rebel artillery began its work, firing solid shot into the blue-coated ranks.

Almaden feared a retreat, but the Federal commander was having none of that. As Pyron should have done, he was sending his troops up both sides of the canyon. His infantry and dismounted cavalry carried out the order with remarkable alacrity. Those reaching the top quickly turned and began pouring fire down upon the Confederate six-pounders and their crews.

The cannoneers could not elevate their weapons sufficiently to reach their foes. Almaden found it hard to tell what was happening in the swirling smoke, but he heard a bugle call. At once, the graybacks began a firing retreat, covering the artillerymen as they worked furiously to haul the cannons back up the canyon.

Almaden knew exactly what Pyron would now do—pull his force back across the log bridge to where the canyon was pinched in a narrow, easily defended bottleneck. He'd likely destroy the log crossing as one might pull up a draw-bridge from a moat.

There were blue coats now in the rocks where Almaden crouched. They ignored him, their attention fixed on the Confederates retreating up the trail. Some stray shots rang near, one ricocheting off Almaden's rock. He pressed himself against the ground, hoping his horse would be spared falling victim to this rain of metal. He closed his eyes, listening, fearing that at any moment he might hear the animal scream.

But he did not. The volume of the gunfire began to diminish as the two small armies moved on past him. From his perch, Almaden watched as the Union infantry pressed forward through the canyon, pausing every few paces to fire, loading on the run. These were very good soldiers, as good as Pyron's and better disciplined.

But then, just down on the road, the thick column of blue-coated infantry began bunching up, and all progress stopped. Pyron had picked good ground. It occurred to Almaden that the fate of all New Mexico might be decided right here.

A tall officer on horseback appeared as if magically on the road, somehow managing to hold reins and two pistols in his hands as his horse bolted forward. Almaden saw another revolver clenched beneath his arm. The din of gunfire and distance was such that Almaden couldn't hear the man's bellows, but he could surely see their effect. The mob of infantry broke loose like logs freed from a jam and began to flow forward again toward the enemy.

The mounted officer rode with them, standing high in his stirrups to observe the fighting ahead, then regained his seat and turned his horse back, cantering by and disappearing behind a shoulder of the ridge. In what seemed only a moment, he returned with a large body of cavalry that he had apparently been holding in reserve. At his exhortation, they drew sabers and galloped off after the column of infantry. The racket by the canyon mouth seemed to increase tenfold, then gradually began to lessen.

Almaden stood straight up now, letting loose a long, slow breath. Pyron's Rebels were retreating once more.

He could hear Union soldiers just below his rock and crouched down behind it, waiting.

Whatever their business on the ridge, they abandoned it. When Almaden looked again, they were scuffing their way down to the bottom. An artillery piece with two men riding its caisson came bumping along the road, then abruptly stopped. Another pulled up just behind it.

But they remained unlimbered. The column of Union

infantry reappeared, marching back from the canyon. They were shouting exultantly and looking little diminished by their fight. The cavalrymen followed. This was no retreat. They moved in orderly, confident fashion.

Behind them, goaded along by Federal outriders, was a large group of gray and brown-clad Confederate prisoners, marching with grudging steps. Almaden guessed their number at half a hundred or more—a significant loss in that Pyron had gone into the canyon with less than half a thousand.

The shadows below him were deepening, the gloom of canyon evening rising inexorably on the slope opposite. The Union commander had won the day but was going elsewhere for the night. Almaden guessed it would be Alexander Valle's Pigeon Ranch.

When the Federal soldiers had passed on and an eerie quiet descended upon the gorge, Almaden finally set about looking for his horse, fearful it had joined the Union Army, though he had trained it not to stray. Unable to spot it, he started to descend to the road, but thought better of that and instead climbed to the very top of the ridge.

His stallion, showing better sense than he had, was just below in a gully, munching brush. Reaching the horse, Almaden paused to take several healthy swallows from his canteen then climbed into the wide, comfortable saddle.

If the Federals were going to the Pigeon Ranch, the Confederates would likely go back to the Johnson Ranch at the mouth of the canyon, where they had left their supply train.

Almaden urged his horse forward. He had much to do.

Chapter 8

THE day was cold despite the bright desert sun, a gusting wind shifting from the west to northwest and back again, stinging Harry's face with gritty sand and a powdery red dirt. He rode One-Eye with head lowered and hat pulled down, and his bedroll over his shoulders in the manner of a woman's shawl.

He had no useful idea now of how far he'd traveled since leaving Leahy, or how far he had to go still to reach Santa Fe. He'd given their only map to Leahy, as it seemed he'd have little need for it. The route was clear if he kept the Rio Grande on his left and the mountains on his right and followed the chain of towns and villages until he got to Albuquerque. There was supposed to be a good road from there to the capital, though the term "good" might be defined differently out here.

The last village he'd gone through was called San Acacia, a collection of adobe huts huddled on the west bank of the river and inhabited mostly by Mexicans and a few Indians. The only Anglos he'd encountered there were the man who owned a little trading post and bar and the drunken Confederate straggler who was its only customer. Neither had had anything useful to tell him.

After that, there were no villages for many miles. The trail shifted to the west side of the river. Except for a lone peak off to the northwest and occasional creeks and arroyos that ran across his path into the Rio Grande, the landscape was featureless. Harry felt as though he were looking across the entire North American continent. He supposed he might go mad, living in a place of such unbelievable distances, beneath such an enormous sky. There was something exhilarating about it, to be sure, but it was a hard country—too hard for the ladylike Caitlin Howard or Louise Devereux. Too hard, perhaps, for a Southern "gentleman" such as himself.

He was well regarded as a horseman—had been held to be the best rider in Virginia's Charles City County. But this journey was taking him beyond his limits. He'd be happy to stay out of the saddle for a month, once he got to where he was going.

There was a flight of many birds off to the north. It startled him to take note of them, reminding him of a time when he'd been a young boy dragooned by his father into going hunting in the marshes near the family's Belle Haven plantation. Harry had had poor eyesight even then, and his every shot had missed, which was just as well, as he'd had small stomach for such "sport." His failure to hit anything had produced a melancholy stare and a shake of the head from his father, who had thought he'd missed on purpose. Perhaps, as he had not realized at the time, that was indeed what he'd done.

These western birds were much larger than pheasant,

and they didn't race away from whatever had spooked them. They hung near in the sky, making lazy circles.

Nearing whatever it was on the ground that was attracting them, he walked One-Eye up a gentle rolling rise, halting at its bouldered top. At the bottom of the slope below was a farm wagon—"buckboard," they called them out here—with two figures on the seat. Nearby was a man on a horse, motionless, looking at the two in the wagon as though waiting for them to do something.

The sudden happiness Harry had felt at encountering fellow travelers drained quickly away, replaced by unease. There were no horses harnessed to the wagon, yet its passengers looked as though they had simply paused in their journey to talk to the rider.

Harry had an impulse to call out to the horseman, but repressed it, uncertain. He had another, increasingly more powerful urge to slip away, recross the river, and continue on his way following the east bank—putting this strange scene far behind him.

But his curiosity would not permit that. Never did. Never would. Finally, taking out one of his .36 caliber Navy Colts, he nudged One-Eye forward.

The horseman below remained as motionless as the two in the wagon, though his mount flicked its tail and fidgeted. The animal wore some sort of Indian blanket beneath what Harry recognized as a U.S. Army cavalry saddle. The rider, who had long black hair down to his shoulders, was not in uniform. He wore a long, belted jacket made of hide and dyed a pale yellow, along with blue trousers and soft, brown leather boots. His hat had a wide brim and high, rounded crown.

He was heavily armed, with a long buffalo rifle in his

saddle scabbard and a large knife and two large revolvers in his belt. Urging One-Eye closer, Henry noted that man's skin was brown and leathery. He seemed an Indian, yet was different in his aspect from all the natives Harry had come across since landing in Texas. There was something oddly civilized about him.

As he came closer still, Harry realized that, if the fellow was of a mind to kill him, there was little or nothing he would be able to do about it now, unless he chose to shoot the man first. Back in Virginia, he'd gone through two entire battles without having shot anyone.

But the rider continued to sit his saddle, motionless, calmly observing the two in the wagon.

They had slumped toward each other, but were still erect, their heads tilted back slightly, as though looking at the sky. They no longer possessed the wherewithal to see it, however. The large, circling birds had been busy. Their clothes were torn open in places, and, here and there, torn muscle and white bone showed through the flesh.

"Dead," said the motionless rider.

"For their sake, I hope so."

The man grunted.

"Did you kill them?" Harry asked.

"They have been dead two days. Maybe more. I come upon them only a few minutes ago."

He had an odd accent.

"And you've been sitting here staring at them?"

"I wonder why they are sitting up like that. They should be knocked over. Bullets hit hard. They were struck several times."

"Unless someone propped them up afterward."

The rider finally turned to look at Harry, his expression unchanged. "Why?"

Harry had no answer. "Did you have a look at the bodies?"

"I look at them since I come here."

"I mean up close. Search their clothing."

"No. They have nothing I need."

"I don't mean to rob them. I mean to find out who they are."

"What difference does it make who they are? They are dead."

Harry had no answer. He wanted to get away from this place. "They have to be buried."

"No."

"No?"

"You don't know who killed them. Maybe it was Indians. They may still be near. Take a long time to dig graves for them."

"What kind of Indians?" Harry asked. He hadn't seen any since the last village.

"Apache. Navaho. Maybe Ute, but we are too far south for Ute."

"We really should bury them. It's the Christian thing to do."

"I am Christian," the man said. Then he touched his reins against his horse's neck and moved away at a walk, heading in desultory fashion toward the Rio Grande.

Harry slowly circled One-Eye around the wagon. In its rear were two chests, both with the locks knocked or shot off and the lids thrown open. Looking closely, Harry saw that they were full of rocks and pieces of iron.

He backed One-Eye away, then turned toward the departing man in the yellow hide jacket, whose horse was still at a walk. Making a quick choice in companions, he decided to abandon the dead ones and spurred One-Eye to follow the long-haired rider. Perhaps he could find someone in the next village to come out and attend to the deceased—paying in gold coin if he had to.

Wherever the next village was.

"Mind if I ride along with you?" Harry asked, as he caught up.

"Do you know where I am going?" the rider asked.

"No."

"Where are you going?" he asked.

"North," Harry said. "To Santa Fe."

"That is a good place."

"Now tell me where you are going."

"To find the army."

"Which army?"

The man made no reply.

"I'm Harrison Raines. From Washington—Washington, D.C."

"Very far from here."

"Yes. And you?"

"I am called Jacques Tantou."

"Are you Indian? Part Indian?"

An angry look came into the man's very dark eyes. "Yes."

"Navaho? Apache?"

"I am Meti."

"What's that?"

"From Canada. Half Indian, half French *Canadien*. Meti."

"What are you doing down here?"

The other kept riding. Harry noticed the jagged slash of a scar across his right cheek and a burn mark on the back of his hand. The grip of his pistol looked well worn.

The sun was still high in the sky. Harry pulled his horse up.

"I'm going back," he said. "Those poor wretched people need to be buried."

He turned his horse and started toward the wagon. Halfway to it, he looked back and saw Tantou not twenty feet behind him.

A sergeant led Almaden to the main house of the Pigeon Ranch, where the Union commander was drinking coffee with two of his officers.

"He come in through the lines," said the sergeant. "Says he's a Union man."

The federal commander, whom Almaden recognized as the many-weaponed mounted officer he'd seen rallying the troops that afternoon, got to his feet and took a step closer, not to shake Almaden's hand, but the better to look at him.

"You're Mexican," he said.

"New Mexican," said Almaden. "I am a member of the Santa Fe town council. Don Luis Almaden y Cortes."

"I'm Major John Chivington. Until the main body comes in from Fort Union, I'm in command here."

"You mean this is not the main body?"

Chivington squinted at him in the lantern light. "How did you get through that canyon? You'd have had to ride through the whole Rebel force."

"That's exactly what I did. When the fighting started,

I went up the hillside. When it was over, I came down again. And then rode here to find you."

"Why?"

"I have something for you."

"And what is that?"

"I know a way to get around behind the Confederates."

Just then there was a hallooing out in the darkness. Almaden heard a horse approaching, and then a shout. A moment later, a soldier rushed in from the shadows.

"Major Chivington, we got a Reb officer come through on a flag of truce."

"What's he want?"

"Not sure."

"Bring him in."

A young Confederate captain, trailing several Union soldiers, appeared. "My commander's compliments, sir. We wish permission to come forward into the canyon to recover our wounded and dead."

"Who's your commander?"

"Major Charles Pyron."

"The canyon's wide open," Chivington said. "There's nothing to stop you, as you must have observed coming through it."

"Major Pyron respectfully requests a truce until 8:00 A.M. tomorrow morning, sir, so that we may proceed with recovering our dead and wounded without fear of attack."

The Union commander gave this quick and decisive thought. "Very well. A truce until 8:00 A.M. is granted." He called to an aide. "Escort this Rebel officer back through our pickets."

Pouring himself another cup of coffee, Chivington watched the Confederate make his swift departure.

"You really want to let them get that close, Major?" said one of his officers. "They could move those cannon of theirs up along with the stretcher bearers."

"Won't matter," Chivington said. "Get the men ready. I'm going to move back to Kozlowski's Ranch."

"That's all the way the other end of Glorieta Pass, sir. You want to give up all the ground we won today?"

"There's sufficient water there. Not enough here for all the men and horses. And I want to be nearer the garrison from Fort Union—if they ever come to reinforce us."

"You're retreating?" Almaden interjected. "Don't you care that I know a way to get around the canyon?"

"Bring this man with us," said Chivington to an aide, indicating Almaden with a jerk of his thumb. He finished his coffee and started toward the door.

"As a prisoner, sir?" said the aide.

"I don't care how he comes," said Chivington, "so long as he comes."

"THIS is a terrible place to camp," Harry said, pulling the saddle off his horse.

They were in a shallow arroyo, perhaps a half mile west of the Rio Grande and the river trail, which Tantou wanted to keep some distance from, so as to avoid other travelers. The cut they were in ran from northwest to southeast, exposing them to the general run of wind. The temperature had fallen with the sun, and Harry was shivering. When he had One-Eye safely tethered, he wrapped his saddle blanket around his shoulders.

"If you didn't want to camp in such a place, you should not have gone back to bury those people," said Tantou.

He'd already tended to his horse and had seated himself against the bank of the arroyo, weapons at his side.

Harry looked over the ground around them as best he could in the dim light. "There's not much to make a fire with."

"We should not make one. It would draw people to us. Maybe the wrong people. Maybe Indians."

Tantou pulled out a long string of beef jerky, broke it in two, and offered Harry half.

"Thank you," Harry said. He had taken some Mexican corn bread from his saddlebags. He gave a portion of that to Tantou. "Don't you consider yourself an Indian?"

"I am Meti." He ate thoughtfully.

"Where would we be by now if we hadn't gone back for those people?" Harry asked.

"In a better place. A pueblo, with water and a safe place for a fire. Maybe a kiva."

"What's that?"

"Holy place—a place for worship. Hole in the ground."

"You've been this way before?"

Tantou nodded.

Harry's back hurt from the digging they'd done. "I keep thinking about that poor woman in the wagon." He munched the jerky, trying to keep the image of the blood-ied, skeletal face from his mind. "Why didn't the birds eat her hands?"

"Because they were tied behind her, where the buzzards could not get. The two of them were tied together at the wrists. That's why they did not fall when they were shot. I cut the bounds while you were digging."

In Tantou's belt was a loaded pistol they'd found in the wagon. Tantou said an Indian would not have left that. A brooch had fallen from the pecked-apart bodice of the woman's dress. Harry had put it with the items he had taken from the San Jeronimo man downriver.

"Where were you coming from when I came upon you?" Harry asked. "North or South?"

"From the west."

"Out in the desert? What were you doing there?"

"Keeping away from trouble."

"You weren't coming up the trail from El Paso?"

Tantou shook his head. Harry studied him.

"You said you were looking for the army," he said. "Which army?"

Tantou scrunched down on the ground, rolling himself in his blanket, turning onto his side, his back to Harry. He said nothing more.

Harry lay down to sleep, drawing his knees up and pulling the blanket close. For a few minutes, he remained wakeful, wondering if he might that day have buried the people who were supposed to help him.

Chapter 9

MAJOR Chivington arrived at Kozlowski's Ranch with his small federal force before sunrise the next morning, less flushed with his victory than wearied from the effort expended for it. Having posted scouts and sharpshooters at the eastern end of the pass—satisfied he had Pyron's Confederates locked up in the canyon—he'd decided to keep his troops in camp at Kozlowski's for another day in hopes that reinforcements from Fort Union might turn up.

So they did, and in short order, a contingent twice the size of Chivington's under the command of a Colonel John Slough.

Through all this, Almaden had been kept under guard, but was treated in gentlemanly fashion—neither bound nor locked up. The patch of ground they gave him at Kozlowski's to rest upon was near enough to the headquarters tent for him to observe proceedings, as Slough and Chivington sorted out their responsibilities and made plans and preparations for the next day. Theirs was not an amicable collaboration.

Slough seemed a ill-tempered man, withdrawn and aloof and giving a strong impression of unease. The soldier assigned to watch Almaden told him that the colonel, a Denver City lawyer, had never been in combat before. Like most of the Coloradans he'd brought with him, he was a volunteer, a raw recruit with an eagle on his shoulder who'd been given the command because of his education and status as a prominent citizen.

Chivington oddly resembled Slough, though he had more bulk and decidedly more of a commanding presence. He had been a church elder back in Denver and had originally been put up to serve the little army as chaplain. But he'd declined that honor to serve as a combatant. Few veterans could have matched the ferocity he'd displayed in the fight back at the canyon. His men obeyed him without hesitation and would be loyal to him the next time they did battle. Slough was another matter.

He'd shown no interest in talking to Almaden, blithely ignoring or disdaining the military advantage Almaden had offered him.

There'd been some New Mexican militia moving about the camp, but no sign of either of his sons, though he had expected both of them to have joined up with the Federals by now. He asked one of the militiamen about them, giving the man a cigar. But the soldier only shrugged, saying he was from southern New Mexico and had not heard the name Almaden before. He promised to ask his comrades if they knew of the two brothers.

After the midday meal, Almaden had gone to sleep on his little patch beneath a tree. He was shaken awake by one of Chivington's troopers.

"Major wants to see you, amigo," the man said. "Let's go."

Almaden sleepily rose, then started toward the headquarters tent. His escort steered him away, however, bringing him instead down to a militia encampment near the Pecos River. There was smoke rising from cooking fires. The smell was of familiar food.

Major Chivington was standing by a militia officer dressed in regulation Union blue, but with several Spanish touches, including fancy boots, a wide red sash, and a wide-brimmed Spanish hat. There were lieutenant colonel's insignia on the shoulders of his short jacket. He was Almaden's age and carried himself like an aristocrat. Which was precisely what he was.

"Manuel!" said Almaden.

The New Mexican officer's face opened in a wide, bright grin.

"So, it is you, Luis!" he said, in Spanish. "I hoped it was you they were talking about. I am very glad to see you well. These days—well, I suppose we have both lost friends."

The officer's name was Manuel Chavez. Like Almaden, he had fought in the Mexican War, only on the side of the gringos and against Santa Ana, whom he considered a tyrant. His family was one of the oldest in the territory and owned more land even than Almaden's. Once enemies, the two of them had become fast friends while still young men and had shouldered rifles together as volunteers mustered to fight off raids by Apaches who'd recurringly threatened Santa Fe and Taos. There'd been talk of marriage between Almaden's daughter, Isabel, and Chavez's son, though Isabel had been pointedly uninterested. Relations between the two families had cooled after that, but the two men remained friends.

"You can vouch for this man?" asked Chivington.

It irritated Almaden to see that an Anglo major serving in a regular Union Army unit apparently outranked a lieutenant colonel of Mexican extraction in the militia.

"*Con mucho gusto,*" said Chavez. "He is one of the first citizens of Santa Fe. On the town council. And loyal to the Union. Are you not, Luis?"

"That's why I am here," said Almaden.

"He says he knows a way to get behind the Rebels in Glorieta," Chivington said. "Can you vouch for that?"

"And what way is that, Luis?" asked Chavez.

Almaden was grateful to have at last come upon men with brains. "An overland trail. It starts near here and runs south of the pass straight across the big mesa. It comes down near the Johnson Ranch. You must know it, Manuel."

"I know of it, yes, but it only goes to the western edge of the mesa. There is no way down from there."

"I believe there is."

"I think you should accept his word," Chavez said to Chivington. "He has lived in this area all his life."

"Your militiamen will come if we attempt it?" the major asked.

"We follow your orders."

"Then I think we should try it," Chivington said. "Fighting in the canyon, we and the Rebs just push each other back and forth. Get a lot of men shot up for nothing."

"What about Colonel Slough?" Chavez asked.

"He'll let us do it—if I push him a little. Maybe if I push him hard."

Without further comment, he left Almaden in Chavez's company and set off for Slough's tent in a determined trudge.

"You have eaten?" Chavez asked.

"*Sí. Gracias.*"

"Will you join me in a drink?"

"*Sí.* But allow me to supply the drink. I have a bottle of excellent tequila from Mexico. They call it '*Osa Negro.*' "

"That I will join you in happily."

They walked up the path to where Almaden's horse was tethered. The bottle was still in his saddlebag.

Though they passed it from one to the other, they drank formally, commencing with toasts to one another.

"I am pleased you have joined us, Don Luis," Chavez said. "We have too many friends who have thrown in with the other side."

"They suffer from the delusion that the Confederates will be our allies," said Almaden, carefully wiping his mouth. "How long have you been with the Federals?"

"From the very moment I learned that the Rebels had crossed over from Texas. I was with them at Valverde. The Union men should have won that battle, but their commander, Colonel Canby, he had bad luck—and missed his chance."

"Is he coming here?"

"I hope so. But I don't think so. I think he's still down in Fort Craig." He took another turn at the bottle. "But that may be to the good. If we win here, and make the Confederates retreat, they could be trapped between our two forces."

"They must be defeated," Almaden said. "So badly that they don't come back. This Confederacy—President Davis—he is in league with those opposed to Juárez."

"They must be defeated," said Chavez, "because they are enemies of the United States." He returned the bottle to Almaden. "Chivington took your weapons?"

Almaden nodded.

"Then let us retrieve them."

Two Union Army privates were guarding the ammunition train where Almaden's pistol and rifle had been put. They declined to salute Chavez, but stepped aside to let him pass, and raised no objection when he returned the arms to Almaden.

"Have you seen my sons?" Almaden asked, putting the pistol into his belt.

"Your sons? Roberto and Eduardo?"

"One went to Fort Union early on to join the militia. The other was supposed to do the same."

"I don't recall their names from the muster. But I will ask."

"You are a good friend, Don Manuel."

"So are you, Don Luis—now that I know you are with us."

HARRY was so weary from his travels and grave digging labors that he slept deeply through the night, despite a bitter wind and a desert cold that greeted him fiercely when he awoke at sunrise the next morning. He lay unmoving, huddled in his horse blanket, for several minutes, his eyes vaguely focused on the mountain ridge to the east. When he finally stirred, stretching out his legs, an assortment of unfamiliar pains beset him from all quarters.

"I am unused to this life," he said to Jack Tantou.

There was no reply. Rolling over, he looked to where the Meti had gone to sleep the night before, but there was no sign of him. No blanket, no clothing, no weapon. Nothing.

Harry sat up, blinking, then put on his gold-rimmed spectacles—amazed that they were surviving this journey and its rigors so well. He looked all about the little riverside cleft where they had camped, finding only his one-eyed horse. Everything of Tantou's, including his mount, had vanished.

He stood up, surveying the full far reach of desert and scrub around him. It was as empty as when they had arrived at this place. There was distant smoke or haze to the northwest, colored a vague orange from the early morning sun. Otherwise, the sky was sharply clear.

Pointlessly, he called out Tantou's name—as loudly as he could find the strength to manage at so cold and early an hour. A few echoes followed; nothing more.

He swore, then, yawning, went about his morning toilet, leading One-Eye down to the river for water and washing his own face and hands briskly. He yearned for a hot bath as much as he did clean clothes, but suspected both would have to wait for Santa Fe. There was no point dressing up for his horse.

Returning to his bedroll, he sat down upon it, wondering hopefully if Tantou had merely gone off scouting—looking for his army or perhaps just fresh meat for breakfast. Harry decided to give the man one hour. If he did not reappear, Harry would continue on alone as he had after parting from Leahy. If things had gone well for them, the Confederate invaders would likely be far to the north—perhaps well beyond Santa Fe. That place was now the object of all his desires.

He breakfasted on bread and jerky, fed his horse from a sack of feed he had bought in Las Cruces, and then saddled him, noticing how much tighter he had to fasten the cinch.

Harry still had a fair stretch of time to wait. He looked through one saddlebag to see if the gold was still there. To his surprise, it was. Then he opened the other bag, taking out a grisly parcel.

It contained all the personal effects of the unfortunate couple. Tantou had kept the dead man's pistol but the rest of the belongings Harry had taken, having decided to give them to the first representative of the law he might encounter, if that proved possible, though it would probably have been wiser to have left these unfortunate legacies with their deceased owners. For a moment, he considered discarding them here—along with the gold coins from San Jeronimo.

But they all now must belong to someone—the gold in particular.

He spread the items out on the ground—a man's wallet, containing a few U.S. greenbacks, the two letters in Spanish, and a pocketknife. There were also a rosary, a woman's Spanish hair comb, an enameled pocket mirror, a locket bearing a portrait of a handsome middle-aged man, a brooch, and a piece of silver and turquoise Indian jewelry that looked as though it was to be worn on a chain from the neck, though there was no chain to be found.

There was another, less appealing object he'd kept: a spent bullet that had passed through the woman's chest and lodged in the wagon seat. It was somewhat misshapen, but not completely deformed. Looking at the base, he judged it to be of .44 caliber—doubtless commonplace in this dangerous region.

Harry had an army surgeon friend back in Washing-

ton—Colonel Phineas Gregg—who had introduced him to
the new French science of ballistics and might have been
able to construct quite a tale about the murdered couple
for him. But Gregg was two thousand miles to the East,
attending to the slaughter in Virginia. Harry would have
to attend to his curiosity on his own.

He returned the items to his saddlebag and stiffly
climbed aboard One-Eye, scanning the horizon again for
Tantou—or anyone.

He was still alone. With a flick of rein, he moved the
horse forward.

WORD had come back from scouts Colonel Slough had
sent up the pass that Pyron had received reinforcements
from Galisteo and was camped at Johnson's Ranch at the
western entrance to Apache Canyon. The Confederate force
had grown to more than a thousand fighting men.

With Slough's Fort Union troops, the Federal army here
now numbered better than thirteen hundred, more than
enough to keep the Rebels from breaking out of Glorieta
and heading north to Colorado.

But, to Alamaden's surprise, the uneasy-looking Slough
had either devised or agreed to a fairly daring plan that
might accomplish much more than that. At last accepting
Almaden's word that there was a highland trail that could
put a Union contingent in the Confederate rear, he'd decided to divide his force in two.

He would retain some eight hundred troops to defend
the eastern end of the pass from the base at Kozlowski's
Ranch, while seven companies under Chivington's command would follow the highland trail over the mesa and

come down in the Confederate rear. Chavez's New Mexicans would take the point.

The object was to trap the Rebels in the canyon and take the whole force prisoner. They would have no choice but to surrender, or fight and die.

Almaden wasn't certain whether Slough fully believed in the plan or wished to put Chivington, by far the better officer, at some distance from his command. But if there was a way to defeat a smart and resourceful commander like Pyron, this was surely it.

Slough left a company to guard the supply train at Kozlowski's, then set out with the main body for Glorieta. Chivington, with Chavez and Almaden riding just ahead of him, led his column due west, passing the ruins of the old adobe church at Pecos.

Only three walls of the structure still stood, but they were an imposing four stories high. Chivington halted his horse to study the relic.

"This was a Catholic church?" he asked.

"Four hundred years old or more," said Almaden. "What's left of it."

"What happened to it?"

"The Pueblo Revolt. The Pueblo Indians of this area rose up against the Spanish. It was in the year 1680. I think they rebelled mostly because they were beaten into practicing the Catholic religion. They killed as many Spanish colonists as they could. The rest fled to El Paso. This church was burned."

"But the Spanish came back."

"*Sí.* But not for another twelve years. Until then, the Indians were free."

"And now they're fighting for the slavers."

"No, senor. I think they are fighting for themselves. If the Confederates win and hold New Mexico, sooner or later, they will fight them, too."

Chivington ordered the column forward. The trail narrowed as they wound up the side of a small hill, and so they slipped into single file. Abruptly, the major halted again, looking at a hole in the ground large enough to corral a dozen horses in. The excavation was perfectly round, lined with a wall of stones.

"And what's that?" he said. "A latrine?"

"No, senor," said Almaden. "That's a holy place. A kiva. An Indian church. They had wooden roofs, but those are all gone. This one, I think, is very old."

"As old as that Catholic church?"

Chavez and Almaden exchanged grins.

"Older," Almaden said. "Maybe eight thousand years. This was once a big Indian city. A trading center. The plains Indians would come down here and meet with the Pueblo Indians. This was a big crossroads."

"What happened to them?"

"Wars. Some with the Spaniards. Some with each other."

"And now this war," Chivington said.

"And someday maybe they ask what happened to us," said Chavez.

HARRY remembered from the map that the Rio Grande curved away to the east at this point, making a wide detour before turning back west again near a village called La Joya. To continue following its course would have meant hours added to his ride through this desolate stretch, so he'd left the river and struck out directly north, taking his direction from the position of the sun. For miles he encountered only a few circling birds and a lone coyote who had sat at a distance, watching him pass. Then the wildlife vanished completely as he found himself in the midst of sand dunes that reached to every horizon like a sea of frozen waves, the wind lifting sweeps of sand much as it might a water spray.

He'd been following tracks. Here and there, he found a lingering trace of them, but mostly they'd been covered by blown sand. It was thick and soft and an annoyance to One-Eye, who slowed his pace and at times stopped completely, resuming his equine trudge only with the goad of spur.

As time passed, Harry began to worry about his course. A miscalculation could take him miles out of his way, or deep into the empty desert. For a panicky moment, he considered breaking off and heading due east to regain the river, but the loss of time might keep him from reaching La Joya before dark. He had no wish to pass another deeply cold night alone in the wasteland. He checked his water supply. It wouldn't do to run out of that, either.

THE trail was just as Almaden remembered, narrow and rocky, cutting steeply across the face of Glorieta Mesa in switchbacks. They were perhaps a third of the way to the top when they heard the sharp reports of gunfire to the north. There was no way of knowing whether Slough had run into a Confederate ambush, or if the opposite had occurred, but the sound became rapid and loud. Within minutes, the boom of cannon fire joined in. For better or worse, the battle was joined, its outcome an open question.

Almaden had stopped, looking off to the narrow valley from which the sounds were coming. Chivington eyed him curiously, then with annoyance.

"Is there something amiss, Mr. Almaden?" the major asked.

"I hope not."

Chavez halted alongside. "There is nothing we can do about that," he said, gesturing toward the unseen fighting.

"Yes there is," said Almaden. "We can get across this mesa as quickly as possible."

It seemed such a long and terrible distance now. He crossed himself and said a silent prayer for the Union soldiers, then spurred his horse back onto the trail.

WELL past midday, Harry came to the end of the dunes. An arid, featureless plain stretched before him. To the northeast, he could see a dark meandering line he took to be the river, judging it to be five or six miles away. There was no habitation in view, but the trail, as though by some magician's command, reappeared on the harder ground ahead. His dead reckoning had proved uncannily precise, though he'd steered One-Eye strictly by guess and a vague measure of the sun's progress. As his gloomy fears began to evaporate, he found himself feeling exceedingly proud. Perhaps he could indeed serve the Union Army as a proper scout, and not simply as a none-too-competent spy.

One-Eye's hooves stirred up plumes of sandy dust as they came down the side of the last dune. The animal stumbled at the bottom, pitching Harry forward onto his neck. The inadvertence may have saved his life, for he just then was further startled by the crack of a gunshot and the whiz of a bullet only inches behind his head.

Spooked, One-Eye took off toward the west, which Harry suddenly realized was, curiously enough, the direction from which the shot had come. He pulled hard on the reins, yanking the animal's head back in the opposite direction, just as two more shots rang out. One-Eye protested with a bolting lunge, and then both horse and rider came crashing down to the ground.

THE sounds of the unseen battle had moved away, fading into the wind. Then, more than an hour after Chivington's column had attained the summit of the mesa and started across its sandy, brushy top, the crackle of gunshots returned, sounding tiny at such distance, but clearly discernible.

Almaden stopped—Chavez, Chivington, and two other officers pulling up around him.

"What is it?" Chavez asked. "Surely we are not lost?"

"No," said Almaden. "The battle has moved."

Chivington nudged his horse nearer. "Moved?"

Almaden pointed to the northern horizon. "Deeper into the pass. I think as far as Pigeon Ranch."

"That's a good sign for the Union," Chivington said. "An advance."

"Yes, I think so. But a better sign would be no battle at all."

"We've come how far?" Chavez asked. "Eight, nine miles?"

Almaden shrugged. "*Mas, tal vez menos.*"

"Only halfway, then?" Chivington asked.

"*Sí.*"

"We must hurry," Chivington said.

HARRY lay in the sand watching One-Eye lunge along the plain, harried by gunshots. Happily, they all missed the frightened animal. More came in Harry's direction, striking just above him. He was grateful for the poor marksmanship.

One-Eye now, for some mad, mysterious reason, stopped completely, and began munching at the dried leaves of a small bush. Harry desperately wanted the horse to escape, though that happy event would cost him his only chance of escaping.

It was said that the Indians sometimes killed travelers for their horses. Here they had a chance to take his mount without having any of the bother of killing him, yet made no attempt to do so. Perhaps their reluctance was owed to One-Eye's lingering within the ostensible range of Harry's firearms. They could not have known how bad a distance shot he was.

Finally, the horse did move away, ambling out of range, off to the northeast, as though he knew that the river lay in that direction. Harry's adversaries were content to let the animal go. He wondered if they were not Indians but bandits— or a Confederate patrol. Whoever they were, they seemed interested only in him. Another flight of bullets thunked into the sand above him, spraying his face with grit.

He pressed closer to the dune. He was in a shallow depression at the base. Though they must have seen him fall, his assailants now apparently could not put him in their sights, a dilemma they could resolve simply by moving themselves and improving their angle.

Rolling carefully onto his back, he took out both his Navy Colts, checking the loads and then turning onto his side, holding the weapons close to his chest. He had an impulse to take a quick look over the bulge of sand and try to gain some small idea of what he faced, but realized that would only clearly mark his location for them.

He tried to think as they might, whether Indians, bandits, or Southern soldiery. It didn't require a Clausewitz. One of them would need only fire off enough rounds to pin him in his spot while the others, or other, moved through the dunes to come at him from the side or rear.

It occurred to him that the bursts of gunfire he'd received were probably an indication that the flanking movement was already under way. He went over onto his back again, squinting his eyes as he searched the top of the dune for what might be the most likely spot his bushwhackers would choose to make their appearance.

He guessed wrong, but a spurt of sand coming of a sudden from a different location gave him warning enough to shift his aim and get off a single shot at the most murderous face he had ever seen.

The head had snapped back, falling from view, but lengths of the man's long dark hair still hung over the edge of the dune. There was no more movement, and the fellow did not cry out.

More gunshots came at Harry, but in smaller volume. If there were more than two of them left, Harry guessed the flanking maneuver would be repeated—only from a different direction.

He could still see his horse, a tiny figure far along the plain, apparently uninjured, continuing northeast. If Harry survived this, there'd be a hell of a lot of walking before he'd meet the beast again.

Survival. A ludicrous imagining. His doom was as certain as the sundown, but it would be far quicker coming. He stared at the dune above him, trying to calculate how much time he'd have to fire. He was as good as dead. This pile of sand was his grave.

His only chance was to move from this spot. But if he

showed even an inch of himself a bullet would be coming his way an instant later. Had he his hat at hand, he might test that possibility, but it lay a good twenty feet distant.

Harry made a calculation. A hat was a big target; his hand would be a small one, even with a pistol in it. The shooter would have to be a very excellent shot to hit him. It was worth the risk—if he still had time to attempt it.

Cocking the weapon, he lifted the Colt in his right hand up over the bulge of sand and fired off a shot, keeping hand and pistol visible for a few seconds afterward.

There was nothing in response. For a moment, he was gripped by the mad, desperate thought that his assailants had decided to depart—having already lost one of their own number. But that was a foolish, wishful notion. What was doubtless happening was that they were now moving through the dunes, presuming he'd stay where he was, persuaded he was pinned down when actually they had given him a chance to move.

This was probably a foolish, wishful notion as well, but the gambler in him elected to take the chance, if only because it gave him his best odds. Without further thought, he pulled his knees up close to his chest, dug his heels into the sand, then shoved, thrusting himself backward out of the little bowl of sand. When no shot came, he glanced quickly about, then, at a crouch, scurried from that dune back to the shadow of another.

Listening, he heard only the wind. With care, he slowly raised his head. He saw nothing but dune, then the sudden, close crack of a rifle or pistol shot kicked up a spray of sand and dust right in front of his face.

Blinking it from his eyes, he crunched down, just as two more shots struck beside him—fired from behind!

He turned, bringing his Colt to bear but realizing he was

too late. Another dark-haired man with headband and long jacket had risen just behind him—tomahawk in one hand; carbine in the other. He threw the tomahawk before Harry could fire, raising his rifle in almost the same motion.

The weapon struck Harry in the meat of his shoulder, a glancing blow that nevertheless tore his coat and skin and shuddered him with pain. His pistol went off unaimed, the bullet whizzing into the air. Then there were two more gunshots, fired at some distance.

Recocking his weapon, Harry watched in stunned amazement as the tomahawk thrower pitched forward, plunging face forward into the sand and not moving thereafter. Someone else had killed this man.

More gunshots. He whirled around, but saw no one. Two more, and then one. And then stillness again.

Harry inched backward, toward the dead man, while keeping his eyes on the near horizon. Directly in front of him, a head appeared. Harry swung his Colt to the fore, then his hand began to shake. He lowered the weapon.

"Tantou," he said.

CHIVINGTON had taken to consulting his pocket watch at increasingly frequent intervals, checking its measure against that of the sun, which had begun its afternoon descent.

"You're sure we're on the right trail, Mr. Almaden?"

"Yes, Major."

"The distance we've come—it's a good day's march for an army."

"The day is far from done, Major," said Chavez. "And we're almost there."

"You have said that several times now."

Almaden reined in his horse, then pointed to the horizon. "You see those mountains, senor?"

"Yes. Do we have to go that far?"

"No. Those are the Jemez Mountains. Between them and us is a broad valley. The Rio Grande runs through it. The near edge of that valley is at the foot of this mesa. You see, there is nothing but the near horizon, that line of brush there, and then the distant Jemez."

"What is your meaning, sir?"

"We are within two miles of where we want to be."

Chivington stood up in his stirrups and looked all about him, then turned and barked out orders to the small staff riding behind him. Outriders went galloping off to the right and left. Three scouts were sent forward, raising dust as well. When they were perhaps a quarter mile ahead, Chivington raised his arm and then gave the signal for the main column to advance. He motioned to Chavez and Almaden to stay close, and they went forward together.

Accepting Almaden's word that their path would take them to the western end of Glorieta Pass, Chivington had devised a simple plan. It was to descend from the bluff, take control of the mouth of Apache Canyon, and in one swoop cut the Rebels off from their base at Santa Fe. Once that was accomplished, they would then push eastward into the canyon until the two segments of the Union army had the Confederates under fire from both ends and trapped between them.

What they found at the edge of the mesa depressed them all. The trail to the valley below was far too steep and dangerous to take horses down. Peering down the gravelly, boulder-strewn slope, almost sheer in some places, they weren't certain how reliable the way was for soldiers on foot, either.

But, however they made the descent, an enormous prize awaited them at the bottom. There, at Johnson's Ranch, just the other side of a line of trees, was a sea of supply wagons. Almaden gave up counting after fifty, estimating there were eighty or ninety of them—maybe a hundred, for some were doubtless hidden from view.

If these wagons and mounds of supplies could now be seized and destroyed, the Confederate Army that had conquered so much of New Mexico would be rendered impotent—helpless. Chivington's small body of men could serve as a knife drawn across the Rebel throat.

Crouching down so as not to be visible to the Rebels below, Almaden and Chavez surveyed their position. Farther along the bluff, dismounted and kneeling by a mesquite bush, Chivington was doing the same with his field glasses. When he lowered them, he gestured for Almaden and Chavez to join him. Several of Chivington's Union officers came up as well.

"They don't see us," Chivington said. "I don't think they have fifty men down there. I mean to take that place."

"How do we get at 'em?" a young officer asked.

Chivington looked to Almaden. "Is there a horse trail?"

"Yes. But not nearby. Miles to the south."

The major rubbed his moustache for a moment, a ritual that accompanied thought. "We'll attack on foot. I want all the rope you can find. Leather straps. Anything that'll get us down off this mesa."

CHIVINGTON left half a company of men on the mesa to guard the horses. The main body lowered themselves to the valley below with the ropes and leather bindings. The Rebels had posted guards, but most of them seemed to be at the canyon mouth and over by the road to Santa Fe, the mesa ignored as just another feature of the landscape with which they'd grown familiar.

Once assembled below, the Union force moved immediately against the foe, two companies assigned to the flanks and the rest charging the center of the wagons. They moved at the double quick, firing as they went, almost immediately capturing a dozen or more of the stunned and bewildered Confederates and then routing the rest. A large group of men they'd seen lying and sitting about the ground near the main ranch house proved to be Union prisoners captured at the fight for Apache Canyon two days before.

Those men were as taken aback by Chivington's arrival as the Rebels had been, though far more agreeable about it, and were very willing to help with the task that now waited.

"Burn it all," Chivington said. "Every wagon. Everything."

"What about the animals?"

There were indeed some eighty wagons, and more than five hundred horses and mules, many of them presumed to be the mounts of Rebel cavalry who'd gone into the canyon on foot. Almaden was revolted by the ensuing slaughter, but it was over soon. The wagons were pulled apart and set fire, then the stores were thrown into the flames: food, saddles, forage, tents, clothing, and medical supplies, as well as ammunition. Win or lose in the pass, the Confederates would find nothing waiting for them.

A rider came out of the canyon at a gallop, pulling up as he saw the disaster that had befallen his army's supply train.

"Get that man!" Chivington cried. "He's a courier!"

Two of Chavez's militiamen were the first into saddles, their horses sprinting toward the small rise on which the Rebel rider sat his mount. The Rebel was much too quick for them. With head down, whipping his animal, he sped back into the canyon. The New Mexicans went as far as the canyon entrance, then halted, uncertain.

Chivington told Chavez to wave them back. "Now we cannot surprise them if we go in there. They will surprise us—wait in ambush—cut us down as we come upon them."

"Unless they're too busy fighting Slough and the main body," said one of his officers.

"There's no way of knowing that," Chivington said, returning the pistol he'd had in hand throughout the attack to his holster. "No, we can't do it." He looked to Almaden. "We'll have to go back the way we came."

The burning ammunition was beginning to explode. The smoke was voluminous and rising fast. It would be seen for miles.

"What will you do with the Confederate prisoners?" Chavez asked.

"Leave them with you." Chivington's eyes kept shifting to the blazing wagons and stores. He seemed at once thrilled with what he had accomplished and jittery about what would come next.

"You're leaving us behind?" Chavez asked.

"Only as the rear guard. The rest of us will start out for Kozlowski's."

"By way of the mesa."

"Yes."

"But what about the prisoners? Do you want me to shoot them?"

"Of course not. We're not barbarians. When we have

most of us back on top of the mesa, run those people into the canyon and let them go. You can fire a few shots at them, to encourage their progress, but aim to miss. I want them back with their main body, spreading alarm."

Chavez grinned. Saluting, he returned to his men.

Almaden gave Chivington a slight bow. "With your permission, Major, I would like to return to Santa Fe. I've done what I set out to do. You have no need of me now. I want to get back to my hacienda."

"I sure as hell do have need of you. It'll be well onto dark before we get to the other side of the mesa. You're going to be a guide again, sir, like it or not."

In the far dark distance was a glimmer of light. It would fade, grow brighter, and then fade again. As they came perhaps a half mile closer, three lights could be seen—and then another.

"Bernardo," said Tantou.

"Sir?" asked Harry, not comprehending.

"The village. It is Bernardo. I think those are campfires. Could be soldiers."

"I thought La Joya was the next town."

"La Joya is behind us. So is Contreras. They are on the other side of the river. Have you forgotten?"

"Perhaps I have."

"We should get as far as we can from the sand dunes and the Indians. Bernardo is far."

"I do believe I have noticed."

"Many dangers here. Bernardo is large. Safer."

Harry hurt in his seat and injured shoulder and a variety of other places. One-Eye had an unusually gentle gait, but it was all torture at this point.

"By the time we go to sleep, it will be time to get up," he said.

Tantou made no reply.

"You're sure you missed the one that got away?"

"Yes. I shot at him, but he was on his horse and moving, and so I missed."

"And the two others, the ones you killed—they were Apache?"

"Yes. And the one you killed also."

There was a howling off to the west, answered by another to the south. Harry supposed they were coyotes. Wolves lived in woods and forests and would not be in such a desert as this.

"That was the first man I ever killed," Harry said. "The first in the war."

"You told me you shot someone in Baltimore—with that fine Colt revolver you have in your belt."

Harry swallowed hard. "That was a woman."

"You shoot women, Harry Raines?"

"She was a Confederate agent, and she was about to shoot me. I didn't aim to kill her. I aimed away. She was hit by a ricochet. It caught her in the neck."

"You were lucky. Only a fool aims a gun not to kill."

"I don't feel lucky. When I think about it, I'm always sad."

They rode on, Tantou moving into the lead.

"You know what you have done?" he said.

"Something foolish, no doubt."

"You have told me you are a Union man. You speak like a Southern man. But you are a Lincolnite. I think maybe you are a spy. A Federal spy. Here, far inside Confederate territory."

Harry made no response, wishing he could see Tantou's face.

"You trust me, Harry Raines?"

"I suppose I do. You came back and saved me from those Apaches."

"I didn't go back to save you from Apaches. I went back so that I will have an Anglo with me. A live Anglo. Those Apaches were trying to make you a dead one, so I had to kill them. I wish I had killed the last one, because now he and maybe more Indians may be tracking us."

One-Eye stumbled a bit as they crossed an arroyo.

"Now you've told me something," Harry said.

"No I haven't."

"Yes you have. You said you wanted an Anglo with you. We're deep in Confederate territory, as you said. You're afraid of the Rebels. The army you're hoping to find is the federal one. You were a scout for the Union, Tantou."

"You don't have it right, Harry Raines."

"You deny you scouted for the Yankees?"

"No. I don't. But it was not for these Yankees."

"What other Yankees are there?"

"I do not want to talk about this anymore."

It was nearly ten o'clock when Chivington and his men finally descended to Kozlowski's Ranch again, where they were greeted with hurrahing from Slough's troops. The soldiers said they had feared that Chivington's contingent had been captured or killed, which meant they would be outnumbered should the Rebels come back the next day.

Chivington, with Chavez in tow, went to Slough's tent to explain that he did not expect there would be another fight. Left behind, Almaden found a place by a campfire.

He was about to wrap himself in his blanket and let his bone weary body fall into sleep, when Chavez returned, grinning.

He seated himself on the ground next to Almaden, producing another bottle of tequila. He took a drink, then passed the bottle to Almaden, laughing.

"That fool Colonel Slough thought he had lost today's fighting," he said, shaking his head. "He left Pigeon Ranch in the possession of the enemy and retreated back here. On the way back, a Confederate ambulance flying a white flag overtook Slough's column. Alexander Jackson was in it. You remember him?"

Almaden nodded. Jackson had been territorial secretary of New Mexico before deserting to the Confederate cause.

"He's a major now. Assistant adjutant general of Sibley's army. He asked for a truce until noon tomorrow and Slough assented. Damn fool. The Rebels had found out about our burning their wagon train. No food. No ammunition but what they have with them. That's why they wanted a truce. They'll be leaving Glorieta far behind them, as fast as they can go. Heading south."

"Not far enough, I think. They will stop in Santa Fe and loot for what they need. They will do worse than that. They're Texans, most of them. They behaved badly when they came in as conquerors. Now, having lost—they will be unspeakable, vindictive. Slough should have pursued them—captured as many as he could and run the rest out into the desert."

"A dispatch rider has come in from General Canby down at Fort Craig," Chavez said, smiling. "Had an unpleasant message for Slough—a complaint that Slough disobeyed orders by leaving Fort Union to come here and engage the enemy on his own."

"But we outnumbered the Confederates. And we won!"

"No matter. Slough is shaken. He looks very bad. I think he is afraid."

"Of what?"

"Of his own men. I'm told one or two shot at him during the battle. They want Chivington as commander."

"I would, too."

"They won't get him. Canby said he is coming up here from Fort Craig to take command. He's bringing all his men."

"That's crazy. The Confederates will be going south."

Chavez drank, then passed the bottle. "Maybe they will run into each other."

"This war is so stupid."

Chavez laughed again. "It's the only one we have."

"But Manuel, you know that is not true."

Chavez's happy glow dimmed a little. "You mean, Juárez's fight?"

"Sí."

"That is not a concern of mine, Luis. I am an American."

They fell silent and sat drinking, staring into the fire.

"You are certain you have not seen my sons?"

"I'm sorry, Luis. No."

"Eduardo was going to Fort Union."

"I am sure they are fine, Luis. They were not with us here. They were not in the battle. So they must be okay."

Almaden frowned. "Maybe they are back in Santa Fe."

Chapter 10

As he followed the Santa Fe Trail north into the capital, Almaden wished he had waited and returned home with the Union Army. The Confederates had pulled out of Glorieta Pass as quickly as expected, leaving their wounded in the canyon instead of taking advantage of the truce they'd been granted to move those unfortunates to safety.

But, if in headlong retreat, they'd lingered long enough in Santa Fe to do their worst. Almaden passed the still-smoking ruins of two houses on the southern outskirts of town and signs of another looting rampage all the way to the central plaza, where he found two women with torn clothes washing themselves at the fountain. He offered to escort them to their homes, but they said they had no wish to go there until the federal soldiers returned. This made little sense to him, but he pressed them no further.

The main door to the Palace of the Governors hung open. Stepping within, Almaden found the building empty. He was surprised at the extent of the theft and destruction. What the Texans couldn't carry out of the place, they had smashed. Perhaps they had decided they would never come back and wanted to show their contempt. If so, their departure was worth the damage.

The long building's interior courtyard, protected from the wind, was warm and sunny. Almaden went out into it, taking some torn papers he had found on a desktop and seating himself upon a small stone wall to read them.

They were written in English, a surveyor's report commissioned by the territorial government some four months before, concerning a prospective road to the north of the city. Almaden studied the map that was drawn on one page, finding nothing of interest.

He heard his horse whinny. Putting aside the papers, he went quickly outside in fear that some Rebel straggler was helping himself to the animal, but found the mare unmolested, if nervous and irritable. That was his own mood as well.

Climbing into the saddle, he took a circuit around the plaza, looking for any sign of his friends, but found none, whether Union or Confederate in sympathy. Deciding to put off his going to his own house, he turned the mare down a street leading toward the Mission of San Miguel, feeling duty bound to make certain that Mercedes had survived the occupation in good health and spirit. Her Southern loyalty would have been small protection against the kind of rampage these Texans had been on. Her friendship with Pyron was another matter, but Almaden doubted that the officer had spent much time in Santa Fe after his defeat. He would be on the road to Albuquerque, or someplace farther south, with the main army, preparing a defense or counterattack. Almaden suspected most of the damage in Santa Fe had been perpetrated by stragglers.

He found one lying in the street outside Mercedes's house, a scraggly bearded fellow wearing cavalry trousers and a buckskin jacket. Almaden was uncertain whether he was wounded or drunk. Dismounting, he found the man to be both. He had been shot in the leg and held a pistol in one hand. A spilled bottle of some kind of liquor lay near his other side.

Someone else would have to attend to him. Almaden went to the wooden gate in the adobe wall of the Beignet house, finding it still barred. A shout drew no one to it. Then at last he heard a woman's voice, telling him in Spanish to be patient. There was a grating sound as the bar was pulled free on the other side, and then a thump as it was set upon the ground.

The door opened only a few inches. It was Mercedes's housemaid.

"Is Madame Beignet at home?" he asked.

"No, senor."

"Is she in Santa Fe?"

The maid hesitated.

"I am her friend. You know me."

"She is in the town, senor, visiting another friend."

"She is all right? Unharmed? You are all safe and well?"

"*Sí.*"

"Would you tell her I have returned and am going to my house here in Santa Fe. Later I would like to call upon her."

"*Sí*, senor. I will tell her."

Before he could speak again, she closed the door. He listened as she hefted the heavy bar herself and slid it into place, then he touched his horse's flank with his spur.

*   *   *

THE stable gate at his house on the east side of town was closed, but unbarred. Pushing it open with his foot, he rode the stallion through it, dismounting in the courtyard beyond. No one came forward to take the horse from him, so he led it into the stable himself, unsaddling and unbridling the animal and putting it in one of the stalls. They were all empty.

The departing Confederates had taken most of the feed, but he found a half-filled bucket of grain and gave it to the horse. Then, gathering up his saddlebags and weapons, he crossed the courtyard to the main house.

This door was unlocked as well. Stepping inside, his footsteps sharp on the stone floor of the main hall, he went to the large front parlor, and then to the smaller parlor, then through the dining room to a back bedroom, then across the hall to a sitting room, and finally to his study. The house, completely deserted, looked exactly as he had left it. Even the crucifix was back in place.

He called out, getting no response.

Returning to the courtyard, he crossed to the kitchen adjoining the stable, finding the central table bare and clean. Going to the oven, he found it cold to the touch.

"Senor?"

Almaden froze, then turned slowly, not wanting to show his alarm. There was a man standing in the doorway, a silhouette against the late morning sun.

"Anselmo?"

His friend and retainer stepped into the chamber. "It is good to see you back, Don Luis. To see you well."

"And you, Anselmo. But where is Isabel? Where is she? Where are the men you were to meet?"

"She is in Peralta."

"By herself?"

"She sent me back. With this letter." He reached into his jacket pocket, unfolding a piece of stationery and handing it to Almaden. "She had an encounter in Peralta, but not with the federal agents you spoke of."

"Did she say why she was not coming back with you?"

"*Sí*. She said she was going to wait for the federal agents—as you commanded."

Almaden read the letter quickly then refolded it. "Did you look at this?"

"Yes, Don Luis. Your daughter did not tell me not to, and I thought it best if I somehow lost the letter so that I could give you the message no matter what. Would you like me to prepare you a meal? The servants are all out at the hacienda."

"Yes. I would appreciate that. Anything you find. I'll be in my study."

"Very good, Don Luis."

Almaden hesitated. "We've won. The Rebels were beaten badly. The Union Army should be here directly."

"I know. The town is recovering from the Confederates' retreat. They came through like rats from a ship."

"And they spared this house?"

"This time, yes."

"Why are the doors unlocked?"

Anselmo spoke as he crossed to the pantry. "The Confederates are gone. Santa Fe is free again."

"Has Mercedes Beignet been here?"

"No, Don Luis." He began slicing bread.

"I'll be in the study," Almaden said. "Make something for yourself. We can talk."

*　*　*

IT was good to be back in his high-backed leather chair. When last Almaden had left this room, he feared he'd never return.

He ran his fingers over some of the objects on top of his desk, pulling close a set of three silver-framed daguerreotypes of his children. Both of his sons appeared nervous and awkward in their stiff poses, as though afraid the camera would wreak some evil upon them, or fearful of the flash powder. Isabel, in contrast, was graceful and composed, a slight smile visible at the corners of her lovely, perfect mouth. She so resembled her late mother it sometimes pained Almaden to look at her. Yet it was always hard to take his eyes away.

He turned in his chair, holding the daguerreotype to the sunlight from the window. She was twenty-three now—well past the age it had been customary for women of her station to marry. He had indulged her in her refusal of suitors from good families, but worried. She was as strong-willed as her mother and had made it very clear that her husband would be someone solely of her own choosing.

There was a click of latch and a creak as the study door opened. Almaden turned toward it, setting the photograph back on the desktop.

"Yes?" he said.

A moment later, he shoved back his chair and went to his knees.

The blast from the shotgun rattled the windows.

Chapter 11

April 1862

THEY had reached a large town called Peralta, which ran for about two miles along the west bank of the Rio Grande and lay directly west of a cut in the Manzano Mountains called Hell's Canyon. They had such pleasanter names in Virginia—Fair Port, King and Queen, Sweet Hall. Nothing about Hell.

Peralta was certainly no Sweet Hall. It differed from all the other places Harry had passed along the Rio Grande only by being slightly larger, possessing two hotels and a theater and a house belonging to Territorial Governor Henry Connelly. There was also a horse trading enterprise, lacking merchandise, and a blacksmith. One-Eye was in need of reshoeing. The smithy, otherwise bereft of customers, attended to his needs at once.

Harry yearned for a newspaper. There were always newspapers back East, but they were as scarce here as clean sheets. The next best thing, of course, was a saloon. Peralta had several, counting the Mexican cantinas. He decided to visit one before obtaining a hotel room. At Tantou's suggestion, they had buried San Jeronimo's gold and some other valuable possessions by some rocks outside of town. Harry left his other belongings in the saddlebags aboard One-Eye. Then he walked to the saloon he had chosen, one patronized by local Anglos.

Tantou said he would wait outside.

"Don't you want a drink? And it's cold out here."

A whipping wind had come up and was blowing sand and old brush down Peralta's main street.

Tantou thought a moment, then, pulling his hat down low, followed Harry inside. It was a dark establishment, the bar, two long boards nailed across the tops of three barrels. There were two tables, both fully occupied with poker games.

No one paid much attention to them as they entered and approached the bar. Harry had been embarrassed at the state of his clothes and appearance, but, looking about, saw that he was by far the grandest looking fellow in the saloon, if not the town. Three Confederate soldiers of ordinary rank stood down the bar to the right. Two ranch hands and a man wearing preacher's garb stood to the left, rolling dice for drinks.

Harry ordered two whiskeys, then turned to the poker games. The larger group was playing seven card stud, boisterously, two of them very much drunk. Only four men sat at the other table, their game, five card draw.

It was Harry's plan to spend the night here, pushing on to Albuquerque the next day. Tantou did not seem to care whether they slept here or in the desert.

"Would you like to try your luck at some poker?" Harry asked.

Tantou lifted his tumbler of whiskey to his lips and sipped. "My luck is that I don't play poker."

"You're sure?"

"Very sure, Harry Raines."

"I haven't picked up a card since I left Galveston," Harry said. "It's kind of an itch."

"Then scratch," said Tantou. He sipped again.

One of the players at the uncrowded table was a Confederate officer—a lieutenant in ragged uniform. He had long, flowing hair and beard, no moustache, and large, protruding, troubled eyes. Harry persuaded himself that his indulgence would be justified by the chance to learn military information.

He excused himself and went to the smaller game, introducing himself as a horse buyer and asking if he might join in. The long-bearded officer observed him speculatively, then grunted his assent. Harry called to the bartender to buy a bottle for the table, then seated himself.

The stakes were low. Harry played cautiously and conservatively, winning two hands but mostly folding. His new companions played glumly, as though they were simply passing the hours of an unpleasant time—which, upon reflection, he supposed they were.

"How goes the war?" he asked, directing the question mostly to the Rebel officer.

The other's oversized eyes lifted from his carefully held cards. "Where you come in from?" he asked.

"Texas," said Harry. Having folded his hand, he poured himself another tumbler of whiskey.

"You don't sound Texan."

"I'm from Virginia. Came out here from Richmond."

"What for?"

"Sell horses to the government."

"You got horses?" said another player, a short, flush-cheeked man in a checked suit who had a large, round belly.

"Looking for them."

Two of the players laughed.

"You got money to buy horses?" asked the officer.

"I draw on a bank in El Paso," Harry replied, lying.

A new hand was dealt. Harry drew two pairs—threes and aces. He decided this was not the best time for a large win and threw away one of his aces with his discards.

He picked up his two new cards and discovered a third three. He simply saw the next bet.

"We got hold of Santa Fe," said the officer, raising the bet and appearing satisfied with Harry's explanation about himself. "If we can keep it, and things settle down, a horse dealer might find some trade. Right now, you're just scratchin' at dust."

Harry saw the bet. He won the pot, but no one seemed too outraged.

"Where're the Yankees?" he asked, raking in his money.

The officer stared at him. "Up in Colorado, lessen we can run 'em out of there, too. Some still over at Fort Craig—too scared to leave."

"You have a garrison here?"

"This is Confederate territory, mister. 'Course we do."

"What you see in here is just about it," said another player.

"We're gonna be a state," said the big-bellied man. "We're joinin' the Confederacy as the state of Arizona."

The dealer halted in mid-shuffle at a sudden sound from the bar—the slam of a fist against the wood.

"Damn Indian!"

Harry turned to see one of the Confederate soldiers walk up to Tantou and lift up the brim of his hat. Standing stiff as a statue, the Meti paid no attention. The soldier might have been an insect not worth the bother of being brushed away.

"You got a damned Indian in here, McGregor!" He gestured at a sign on the wall. Harry could not make it out but gathered it made reference to a prohibition against serving liquor to Indians.

Harry rose from his chair. "He's not Indian. He's French Canadian." His mind raced. "He's my horse handler."

The soldier, unsteady, pulled the hat off Tantou's head. "Look at him! Look at that hair. He's an Indian! Lieutenant! That man brought an Indian in here—and you're playin' cards with him."

"He's not an Indian!" Harry protested, taking a step closer to the confrontation. "He killed two Indians a couple of days ago. I killed one, too. Apaches. Down by the sand dunes south of Bernardo."

Tantou, still almost motionless, and eerily calm, slowly finished his whiskey and set down the glass. He turned around and bent forward at the waist to retrieve his hat. The soldier's boot came down on its crown, fixing the hat in place. Without a moment's hesitation, Tantou grabbed the man's ankle and pulled, hard. He came down like a house wall, his head striking loudly on the wooden floor.

Harry was scarcely able to follow what came next. Two men leapt at Tantou, and then a third. One of them came reeling back. Another was knocked back onto his heels.

Harry thrust himself into the scuffle and was set upon immediately by someone who began pounding on his back, making his shoulder hurt as though it was on fire. He wrenched himself around and found himself facing the Confederate officer from a distance of inches. They stared hard at each other for one or two seconds, then the Rebel tried to land a blow on Harry's nose. Fearing for his spectacles, Harry ducked, causing the blow to strike his forehead instead. There was a gunshot, but no one cried out for being hit. Amidst curses, and clumsy punches, the whole struggling mob of them began to move across the floor, as though glued together.

It was Tantou who was providing the driving power, pushing as he might some mired wagon. One of their adversaries fell off to the side. Another tried to fling himself over a comrade to get at Tantou, failing miserably. Finding himself clear enough to swing his arm, Harry took one of his pistols from his belt and whacked another of their tormentors in the shin. Tantou shoved the last one against a table. Then they both went for the door.

Once in the street, they started for Tantou's horse, but the now very angry group of men they'd been fighting exploded through the door, spreading out and coming at them from all directions, joined by others. At least two of them had pistols out, but they used them as Harry had his—as painful clubs. Harry managed to fend off the first blow aimed at his head, but it struck his elbow instead, stinging his arm numb. The second blow found his skull. There was a bright flash of light, and down he went.

He came to slowly and fuzzily, his vision returning before his hearing. What came to that sense first was what seemed to be a woman's voice—musical, but urgent and sharp. Yet he could see no women, only disagreeable male faces. It then occurred to him that she was speaking from somewhere near, but behind him.

Very near. His head was resting on something very soft. Blinking, he opened his eyes as wide as he could and tilted back his head. There, seen upside down, was a lovely woman's face, somewhat contorted with anger and distress, but perfect in all regards. Her beauty was such that, had someone told him she was an angel descended from Heaven to rescue him from his distress, he would have set his skepticism regarding organized religion aside and become a true believer.

The woman was not looking at him, but at the grimacing men circled around them. It then occurred to Harry that she was speaking in Spanish and possessed a vigorous command of her language. The grimacing men were greatly impressed with her remarks. They of a sudden drew back, stepping aside.

Walking up to Harry where he lay was a leathery, darkskinned, much-scarred Mexican gentleman who might have been mistaken for a criminal were he not wearing upon his grimy leather vest a dented and tarnished badge denoting some manner of law enforcement authority.

"He attacked Lieutenant Holt, Sheriff," said one of Harry's assailants. "So did the Injun. In the bar. This one brought the Injun into the bar and bought him whiskey. Then they set upon us."

The Mexican man with the badge ceased his look-over of Harry and his injuries and spoke to the woman in Spanish. Then he stepped back.

"Bring them," he said, to one of the men.

Harry started to get to his feet, but the use of these

appendages was denied him, as two of his assailants took them in hand and began to drag him unceremoniously across the street, clouding his head in dust. Turning to the right, he saw Tantou being treated to similar indignity. Tantou bore it better, for he appeared to be unconscious.

THE sheriff's office hadn't a proper jail. The adobe building it occupied had apparently once been a store, and what had been the storeroom—a dark, dank, dirt-floored chamber with a small, barred window—served as the detention chamber.

It smelled badly of its previous inhabitants, who'd been afflicted with some digestive distress, among other complaints. Harry had quickly abandoned the rude bunk he'd been assigned, propping himself in a corner instead. Tantou, who'd awakened only briefly, slept on the floor.

This was the third occasion in his relatively brief tenure as an agent of the U.S. Secret Service in which he'd found himself in jail. He hoped the other operatives in Mr. Pinkerton's employ were better at their work.

AFTER several hours, the sheriff brought in a bucket of water and a tin cup, along with some cornbread wrapped in greasy paper. Harry attempted to interest Tantou in it, but the Meti shook his head and went back to sleep.

When next the tranquility of their little dungeon was disturbed, it was well into the night. The door opened with a loud creak, admitting the golden glow of lantern light. The bearer of the lantern stepped quickly inside, closing the door tight. It was not the sheriff, but the Spanish-speaking young lady in whose lap Harry had too briefly rested his battered head.

She sat down on the floor—cross-legged, in Indian fashion—before Harry could rise.

"Senorita," he began. "It is 'senorita,' isn't it?"

"*Sí.*"

"I believe you will not like it in here."

"No. But neither do you, is that not so?"

"That is very much so. My name is Harrison Raines. The gentleman sleeping is my friend Jacques Tantou. I call him Jack."

"I am Isabel Consuelo Maria Theresa Almaden y Cortes."

He thought he detected a small, sweet smile, but in the dim, flickering lantern light, it was hard to be sure.

"What brings you to our humble abode?" he asked. "And how did you get in here?"

"I told the sheriff you worked for my father and had been sent here to assist me. My father is an important man—a man of much reputation in this part of New Mexico—and the sheriff is respectful of him. He is really only the deputy. The actual sheriff left to join the Union soldiers when the Confederates came. There is not much this deputy can do for you, but whatever he can do, he has told me he will do it. He started with admitting me to your horrible quarters."

"I'm delighted you could come—but why did you?"

She leaned close to look at the marks the fight had left on his face, touching his cheek briefly with the palm of her hand.

"You are in very serious trouble. You assaulted a Confederate officer. In their army, that is a hanging offense."

Harry peered closely at his pocket watch, curious that

it hadn't been taken from him. "Then why haven't we been hanged?"

"The lieutenant you attacked is not of high rank. The sheriff persuaded him that he must get permission from a much higher-ranking officer to carry out a hanging. He is looking for one now."

"What wonderful news you bring."

"Be content that they do not know your true occupation. The lieutenant would not hesitate one moment to hang you were he to learn of that."

"And what is my true occupation?"

She lowered her voice, almost to a whisper, and leaned nearer yet, filling Harry's nostrils and spirit with the scent of spicy sweet flowers. "You are a spy. A Union spy."

Harry studied her, wondering if she'd been sent there for the sole purpose of extracting that very admission. "And what makes you think that?"

"My father sent me to find you and help you—to bring you up to Santa Fe. He said there would be two of you and that I would know you when I saw you. I thought he was crazy as I never have seen you before. But now I know what he meant. You have been here less than a day and already you are in trouble with the Confederates. You must be the Union spies we were told were coming."

Harry nodded toward Tantou. "He is not any spy. He's an army scout, trying to get back to his unit."

"But father said there would be two of you."

Fearing he might endanger Leahy, Harry hesitated, but then decided to trust her. He had no one else to trust, or look to for help. "There were, but the other of us struck out for Fort Union on his own, to warn of the Confederate advance."

"He will have been much too late. The Confederates have advanced very far. But maybe they soon come back."

"How do you know that?"

"My father had a plan to make that happen."

"I see."

"Alas, that will not be good for you. I think they may hang you then pretty quick. We will have to get you away from this place."

She spoke as though she had the power to send him to the moon if she chose to.

"I won't object," he said.

Her eyes went to the small, high window. In an instant, she was on her feet, and in another, had jumped upon the cot and was peering outside.

"What's wrong?" Harry asked.

"Gunshots," she said.

He hadn't heard them, but now he did.

"A battle?" he asked.

"No," she said. "I think they are celebrating—like cowboys."

She hopped down again, putting her hand on his arm. He winced.

"Do you hurt?" she asked.

"A little."

"I will come back for you. Be ready."

Chapter 1 2

THE deputy had absented himself, though they knew not where nor for how long. After a hurried search of his little office, they recovered their weapons, which had been piled beneath an Indian blanket in a corner.

Harry caught the girl's arm as she started to open the front door. "Pardon, senorita. Where should we go?"

"I don't know," she said. "Out into the desert. North, to find the Union soldiers."

"What do you think, Jack?" Harry asked.

The Indian had not spoken three words since their arrest. "Find an empty house. Wait for the Federals."

"Perhaps a stable," Harry said. He opened the door a crack, then wider, so he could peer around it and survey the street. "Where are our horses? I left mine at the black-smith's."

Isabel shrugged. "I think the deputy took them both—to his house."

"And our saddlebags?"

"They must be with the saddles."

"Where does the deputy live?"

"I don't know. But we should hurry. Before he comes back."

Harry stuck his head out farther. "There are several soldiers down the street. Perhaps a dozen."

"Yes?" said Isabel.

"There were only four in the whole town when we came in."

"I told you. Their army is coming back. There will be more here soon."

"Where can we go?"

"There is one house I know will be empty. It is just outside the town."

THIS proved to be the house belonging to Governor Connelly. A substantial residence with an encompassing adobe wall and several outbuildings, it sat near the river about a mile north of Peralta.

Both front and rear doors were locked, a challenge Tantou met by breaking an unshuttered window in the back. There was food inside, and wine, though no water. Isabel suggested they hide themselves upstairs, where they would have a greater view of the surrounding countryside and anyone approaching. Harry agreed. Tantou said nothing.

They settled on a back bedroom with a window that opened onto the roof of the rear porch. From it, one could see the Rio Grande and the north road for a long distance. Harry suggested to Isabel that she take the small rope bed. When she only stared at it, and then at him, he bowed to her and seated himself on the floor by the window, leaning back against the wall.

"I'll keep watch," he said.

Tantou stretched out on the floor beside the bed and was instantly asleep.

Finally, she sat upon the counterpane. "The sun will be up soon. We will then have no choice but to stay here all day."

Her face, limned by the dawn, reminded him of a painting he had seen once in New York. A very old oil painting of a young girl. There was the same calm, the same repose.

He could not remember the last time he had looked upon a painting. Isabel would certainly suffice in the meantime.

"We were supposed to exchange words," Harry said.

"We have."

"No. I mean two words. I say one, then you the other. Those were my instructions."

"What other word?"

"You're supposed to know. My word is 'Lincoln.' "

"That's your word?"

"Yes."

She was puzzled, and then was not. "Then I should say 'president?' "

"No. Another word." He waited.

"I do not know it. My father said nothing about this." She drew her knees up to her chin, wrapping her arms around her legs and looking at him unhappily. "I am sorry. I hope you will not now shoot me."

Mr. Pinkerton had given him no instructions for this eventuality.

"My dear lady. I would shoot the man who even suggested I do such a thing."

She looked at him, not unfondly, then lowered her face to her knees, as if resting.

"It's 'Juárez.' " Harry said.

Her head came up. "What did you say?"

" 'Juárez.' That's the word you were suppose to say. 'Lincoln.' Then, 'Juárez.' "

"How do you know about Juárez?"

"He's a Mexican politician. Someone Lincoln knows."

"I know who he is." She rose. "I think I should go now."

The room was turning gray with the increasing light.

"Will you be safe?" he asked. "They'll be looking for us. If they find you . . ."

"I will be safe."

"Where are you going?"

"Maybe I can find your horses."

"I'm betting they'll be gone."

She fidgeted. "Any horses."

"You'll be recognized. You are richly dressed. And, if I may say so, very beautiful. Very noticeable. If you go into the town and that churlish Rebel lieutenant sees you . . ."

There was an Indian blanket on the bed. Isabel pulled it up around her shoulders and head, then kicked off her shoes.

"Now I am only a peasant woman. Good-bye."

"I should go with you."

"No. They'll put you back in jail."

"Will you be back?"

"I hope so. Maybe." She left the room and went down the stairs without making a sound. Harry returned to the window, but there was nothing to be seen of her, or anyone.

He waited, yawning. The first glint of sunlight reached a streak of cloud. Looking to the horizon, he saw something else.

"Tantou."

The Indian stirred, but said nothing.

"Tantou!" Harry nudged him sharply with his foot.

The other man opened his eyes as a ship might its gun ports. "What do you want?"

"The girl has left us."

"I know. I heard you." The eyes closed.

"I see horsemen coming."

"How many?"

"A lot. I think it's the Confederate army."

"They are coming from the south?"

"No. From the north. I think they're coming back from Santa Fe."

Tantou rolled over. "Good. Maybe they will keep going."

THEY did not. Within a few minutes of the horsemen's arrival, there was a thump and clatter downstairs, and then loud male voices. They did not sound angry, and their business did not appear to include searching the premises— at least not upstairs.

Yet.

Tantou was now at the window, having gathered up his weapons. He put a finger to his lips then pointed outside and then up at the ceiling.

"The roof?" Harry whispered.

Tantou nodded, then proceeded out the window. Harry followed, carefully.

Like most of the adobe buildings in the town, the roof of the Connelly house was flat. Harry and Tantou crawled to the center of it, to remain out of view from the ground. It was becoming warm in the rising sun. As they dared not talk, Harry decided they might as well sleep until dark, and lay back, closing his eyes.

But his mind was unwilling. Images of the dead people he had encountered along the trail from El Paso came and went and then returned and then refused to leave.

The man on the sand-colored horse had been heading south with a thousand Yankee dollars in gold coin. Where was he going, and what was he going to buy with so much money? If he had stolen it, why? He had the look of a very rich man—had the horse of a very rich man. Was he taking the money into the Confederacy, or away from it?

These and other questions batted around his mind like noisy birds—settling on no answers. If he could look again at the man's possessions that he had put into his saddle-bags, he might find a clue. Especially the letters, which the girl Isabel would be able to fully translate for him.

He sat bolt upright.

"Get down," whispered Tantou.

"She's related to them, Jack. Isabel is. The name on those letters was Almaden y Cortes. The letters we took from the dead man."

"If you do not lie down, you will join them very quick. *Bien sur.*"

Harry did so. He wished he knew where the girl had gone.

SMELLS of cooking awakened Harry. Crawling to the edge of the roof, he saw smoke rising from the kitchen chimney and observed soldiers setting up tables in the courtyard. There were a number of officers standing about, and for a moment Harry thought this house had been turned into the Confederates' headquarters. Continued observation led him to a different conclusion, however. They were preparing the place for a party. If the Rebels were on the run, they were feeling celebratory about it.

He eased away from the edge.

"They're preparing some sort of Rebel fiesta," Harry said.

"They are crazy."

"If we wait until they're all drunk, perhaps we can remove ourselves from this place."

Tantou was staring straight up at the sky. "You are crazy. We must wait here for the Federals."

"But what if they don't come?"

"If they weren't coming, these soldiers would not be here."

By nightfall, the courtyard below was crowded with gray and brown uniforms and the black garb of local citizenry. There were ladies among them, and musicians—playing waltzes and fandangos. Feeling safer in the darkness, Harry leaned out over the edge of the roof to gain a fuller view of the merrymaking. He quickly pulled back.

"Tantou. She is here."

"Who?"

"Isabel. She is dancing."

"Like a bear on a chain?"

"No. With one of the officers."

"Do not cut in."

"I need to speak with her."

"This is not the time."

"There may not be another." Keeping low, he moved to

the other side of the rooftop. Two stories below, some soldiers were lounging by the front door of the house. Just to the side was a balcony. If he lowered himself from the edge of the roof and swung to the left, he might be able to land both feet upon it, but not without making considerable noise and causing alarm. If he went back to the other side and tried to regain the small bedroom they'd taken refuge in, he'd be in plain sight of everyone at the party.

Crawling the length of the rooftop, he found only a sheer drop at that end. The same was true of the other. He returned to Tantou.

"I don't know which way to go," he said.

"You cannot go."

"But I must."

"No. Look."

He did, where Tantou indicated, to the north, and also to the east, across the Rio Grande, but saw only night.

"Soldiers," the Meti said.

"They're all over this place."

"No. Different soldiers—across the river. They are waiting. They're Union."

THEY waited all night for the attack. The Rebel officers became so drunk that a squad of Federal infantry could have routed them, but the lurking Union troops did not budge from their shadows.

"Why are they just sitting there?" Harry asked.

"They are waiting for the light," Tantou said. "It is a mistake."

*   *   *

WHEN the fight started, it was the Confederates who fired first, opening the Battle of Peralta with nearly simultaneous shots from two field artillery pieces they had positioned at a wall a hundred yards or more to the north. As the Rebels reloaded, the Union side replied in kind, overshooting their mark but causing mayhem in a barnyard where a company or more of Rebel infantry had been sleeping. More cannon fire followed, contributed by both armies.

Harry lifted his head to better see the battle and was instantly rewarded with the sight of a Confederate column approaching from the north on the Albuquerque road. It contained a half dozen or more supply wagons, escorted by a mounted company and a howitzer. The officer in charge, riding at its head, had almost reached the outer wall of the Connelly compound when he abruptly turned toward the river. Puffs of gunsmoke appeared all along the far bank to greet him. A moment later, a full line of Union soldiery swarmed over it and into the river, firing and loading on the run as they charged.

The Federal artillery shells were falling closer to their target now, one landing in the courtyard that had been the scene of the previous night's festivity and exploding with shuddering violence, peppering Harry with little falling bits of hot metal and wood. He beat out one small smoldering spot on his sleeve, then rolled over to speak to Tantou, who was lying on his stomach, surveying the battle coolly.

"The Federals will win," he said. "But it will take awhile."

Another cannon shell exploded, this one on the other side of the house. In the courtyard, several wounded men were screaming. An officer limped along, trying to pull on his pants and bark out orders at the same time. Several others followed, in similar disarray.

"Now's the time to get out of here," Harry said.

"Better to wait until the fighting is over," Tantou said.

A cannon ball—solid shot—came whizzing overhead, striking a nearby cottonwood tree. A horse whinnied— from fear, or worse. Harry thought of One-Eye, hoping he was being spared this.

"Our fighting will be over for good if we don't get off this rooftop quick," Harry said.

"When the blue coats take the town, then we will be free of these people."

Another solid shot removed the house's chimney with a tremendous crash, leaving a veil of adobe dust in its wake.

"I'm not going to wait," Harry said. "Hope to see you soon, Jack."

Without further hesitation, he swung over the edge and dropped onto the porch roof, hurrying to the open window of the bedroom they had earlier abandoned and diving within, fearing bullets would follow.

He was ignored. The room appeared to be much as they had left it, though Isabel's shoes were gone. He surmised she had retrieved them during the party. That she hadn't betrayed him and Tantou on that occasion he supposed was a good sign—though it may have been only that she believed they had fled the premises.

There was a chamber pot beneath the bed. He paused to make use of it, then went to the stairs. Below, some of the Rebel officers were still emerging from their stupors. One was staggering up the stairs. A third of the way up, he faltered and fell back again.

Across the hall, a door opened with a sharp bang and a

Rebel captain, eyes bleary and reddened, stumbled forth with his arm around a Mexican woman.

"What's all this damned shooting?" he said, wincing at the sound of a shell bursting just outside the house.

"We're under attack," Harry said, choosing his words carefully. "The Union Army. They're coming across the river."

The captain swore, releasing the woman, who quickly stepped back, folding her arms across her chest. She was wearing only undergarments.

"Who are you, sir?" the officer demanded.

"Harrison Raines, of Belle Haven Plantation, Charles City County, Virginia."

"What in perdition are you doing here?"

"I came from the War Department, in Richmond." That was absolutely true, though the circumstances were hardly what he hoped the man would assume. He had left the Confederate capital a fugitive, barely escaping with his life.

The sound of musket fire could be heard now, steadily increasing in volume.

"Excuse me," said Harry. He pushed past the officer and ran quickly down the stairs.

The house showed signs of both merrymaking and pillage—and now war. A window and a portion of wall had been shot out, giving a view of the courtyard. Harry thought of trying for the cellar, wherever it might be, but discarded the notion, not wanting to be trapped as he had been on the roof.

He leapt across the shattered window sill, clambering over the debris in the yard and hurrying around the side of the house. As he stood there, a man dropped down beside him from the roof above, his boots striking the ground with a thud. He kept his footing.

"Change your mind, Jack?" Harry ducked as a bullet crunched into the wall above him.

The Indian pointed to a clump of trees down a lane from the house. "It's safer there. Let's go."

"An agreeable suggestion, sir," Harry said.

They reached their goal with no interference from the very busy Confederates and only minor impediment from the Union side, coming in the form of a Yankee shell that nearly took their heads off and dropped a heavy tree limb just in front of them. Once in the trees, Harry hunkered down, turning his back to the battle and pulling out a package of small, thin cigars.

He offered one to Tantou, who declined.

"Why did you come down?" Harry asked. "I thought you were going to wait for the Federals?"

"They won't be coming. Not soon. They captured that wagon train and drove some Rebels who were on their side of the river back across into town. But now they sit there by the near bank, coming no farther."

Harry realized the intensity of the firing was diminishing.

"They don't want to fight here," Tantou continued. "They are going to wait for the Rebels to run. Maybe catch them out in the open."

"They have a smart commander," Harry said.

"Maybe. Maybe not. The Rebels aren't leaving."

THE battle subsided to desultory small arms fire and the occasional cannon shot. Harry observed a number of Confederate soldiers lying down on the ground, not from wounds but to take sleep. By midday, it looked like the sure Union victory had turned into an abject standoff. Some Confederates had gotten into the wine again and gave every indication of wanting to resume the party.

Harry had been present at the Battles of Bull Run and Ball's Bluff, both hideous slaughters that had sobered the U.S. capital as nothing in the war. These Westerners were treating this engagement as a lark. He wondered how aware they were of what this conflict was about.

"We've got to get some food," Harry said, looking about the still littered tables in the courtyard of the Connelly house.

"Water, too."

"Wait here."

Harry slipped from the trees and then moved toward the house at a crouch, slowing as he passed near a group of lounging soldiers. Reaching one of the tables without attracting their notice, he found a few long, greasy slices of roast beef on a plate and stuck them inside his coat, next to his once immaculate but now torn and grimy shirt. Searching for water, he found only a nearly empty bottle of wine, and then one nearly full.

He treated both like found treasure. Returning to the clump of trees, he presented his purloined little feast to Tantou with a flourish, then poured wine from the nearly full bottle into the other until their levels were near equal.

Tantou wolfed the meat like some wild creature then lifted the bottle to take a long, thirsty drink. When he lowered it, his gaze was fixed on something far in the distance.

"What's wrong?" Harry asked.

The Meti extended his arm toward the western horizon. "Storm coming."

THEY watched as a dark and angry curtain rose higher and higher in the sky. A few drops of rain ticked against the tree branches around them, replaced by stinging particles of sand that grew thicker in volume as the wind rose. Harry turned his back to it, taking last swallows of meat and drink, then flung himself to the ground, pulling his coat up over his head as Tantou had already done.

The rattle of wind-driven sand against the tree trunks increased in intensity until the sound resembled musket fire. The gusts merged into gale, tearing at his clothes and burning exposed portions of his hands and face with the tiny, scouring grains. A branch broke loose from one of the trees and was blown noisily across the lane. Men ran by them, heading for the town, their shouts swiftly engulfed by the tempest. It was as though the world was coming to an end. Harry desperately pressed himself against the earth, fearing and then expecting that eventuality. He began talking to himself, apologizing to the heavens for whatever trouble he may have ever visited upon his fellow human beings—finding himself madly amused at the irony of having escaped injury of any serious sort in two major land battles and one at sea, only to be doomed to death by nature.

Then, slowly, it began to dawn on him that he might live after all. The pitch of the wind shriek lowered in tone. The merciless stinging abated, and then was gone. Opening his eyes, brushing the sand from his brow and lashes, he saw that darkness giving way to daylight again.

He sat up, keeping his back to the diminishing storm. The sky was clearing. Tantou remained prone on the ground.

"It's ending," Harry said.

Tantou slowly lifted his head, turning and squinting to find the sun in the gritty haze. Then he sat up, retrieving his wine bottle.

"Trés mauvais," he said. "I am glad I do not live in this country."

Harry stood up, turning slowly in a circle. "Amazing."

"What?"

"The Rebels. They're pulling back. The Federals couldn't budge them, but a bit of sand in their faces, and off they go."

Tantou rose. "That is not why."

He started back to the house. Harry followed, thinking they ought to be heading into Peralta instead. The structure was intact, but the rest of the Connelly compound was all shambles and debris, with not a horse now in sight.

Tantou went straight up the stairs, back through to their small bedroom, and out the window onto the porch roof. The dust storm had moved on across the river, obscuring the eastern horizon utterly, but the sandy bank behind which the Union force had positioned itself could be seen with the sharpest clarity. There wasn't a single human figure in view there now. He looked up and down the river, but there was no one.

"Where the hell did they go?" he wondered aloud.

"They've gone back to Fort Craig." Tantou shook his head, sadly. "Many more of them than the Rebels. *Beaucoup de plus.* They could have come through the Confederate line like buffalo through the grass. But they did nothing. Their general has no wish to fight the Rebels. He just wants them to go away."

Harry stepped farther out upon the porch roof, looking south to Peralta. He could see horsemen in the main street, forming up and moving on out to the south. There was smoke from a burning building, but otherwise the town seemed to be largely unharmed.

"They are going away—maybe all the way to Texas."

Tantou grunted and sat down. Harry joined him.

The Meti removed his hat, running a dirty hand through his thick, black hair. "What will you do?"

Harry answered truthfully. "I do not honestly know. Maybe the Union boys will come back."

"You come here with orders?"

"They were vague. I was to scout out the Confederate plans and situation here and get word back to Washington."

"How?"

Harry shrugged. "However I could."

Tantou nodded. "I will stay with you."

Some sound Harry could not hear caught Tantou's ear. The Meti crept to the edge of the roof, peered down, then stood up, his boots just an inch from a two-story fall. He motioned Harry forward.

There below them, standing in the courtyard with three horses, was Isabel. One of the horses was One-Eye.

Chapter 13

HARRY spent much of the rest of the journey northward either looking at Isabel or remembering what he had seen. Women aged and weathered quickly in this country. The ladies of the saloons and gambling emporiums they'd visited in Texas had been mostly in their twenties, but some looked twice that age. Many of the Indian and Mexican women he'd encountered along the Rio Grande trail had faces resembling the wind-worn buttes and cliffs he'd passed.

Isabel, by contrast, was a finely polished work of art— large, deeply dark eyes set with perfect symmetry in a sculpted, well-boned face of a light brown hue. Her black hair was as long as the wild mane of his New Orleans actress friend Louise Devereux, but perfectly brushed and groomed. And, uncannily, on a frontier where most everyone Harry had come upon could be smelled yards off, Isabel seemed so clean.

But this could not last long. She needed to leave this harsh place for one where her beauty might be more coddled and nourished. She was a lady who belonged in New York or Boston or Paris. Alas, she seemed as rooted in this land as firmly as the piñon.

Unlike their night at the Connelly house, she had talked little since leaving Peralta. He'd asked her several times, in several ways, what she had done while he and Tantou were hiding on the roof, how she had hidden their animals, and how she came to be at the Rebel officers' party. She politely told him virtually nothing. And the nearer they got to Santa Fe, the more taciturn she became.

While he'd been locked up, someone had gone through the contents of his saddlebags. The Spanish letters had been read and then jammed back inside the pouches carelessly. But nothing had been stolen. The gold they'd buried was still in the rocks where Tantou had put it. That seemed as much a miracle as their surviving the Battle of Peralta and the sandstorm that had ended it.

He tried to speak to Isabel of the dead couple in the wagon, but she only shuddered and bade him stop. When he told her about the bullet he'd taken from the wagon seat, she said she thought that morbid, making him feel like some barbarian who had no knowledge or care of the delicacy required in discussion of the dead.

Finally, as they rode out of Albuquerque, passing near the Sandia Mountains, he found a subject that drew her out—her family's ties to this land. He asked how strongly she felt about it.

"You are from where, Senor Raines?"

"Virginia."

"And you think of it as your country, do you not?"

"In a sense, especially the western part, by the mountains, where I have a farm."

"How long has your family been in Virginia?"

He knew that fact. "Since 1710."

They rode on a few paces.

"My father's people have been in this part of New Mexico for three centuries."

"They were with Cortés?"

"We are related to Cortés."

"Conquistadores?"

"The Spanish were very cruel and corrupt," she said, as though they were a race alien to her blood. "They pulled down the Aztec Empire and slaughtered much of the population. The officers got rich as best they could, mostly by stealing gold from Indians—even those Indians who fought against the Aztecs on their side. But the ordinary soldiers of Cortés—those who survived—they were paid only twenty pesos a man, for two years' fighting. So they stayed in Mexico. Many of them took Indian wives and settled on the land, from the jungles to the south to what is now New Mexico in the north. We are of those people—a blend of the Indian and the Spanish—a new people. This is their land. Mexico is their land. Our land."

Harry nodded toward Tantou. "What about the Indians who did not marry Spanish? What about their land?"

"I never owned land," said Tantou. "*Jamais.*"

"The Indians sometimes come out and fight us, but for the most part we let them be. It is you people who have come here as conquerors—as takers of land."

"I am a Virginian," Harry said. "We take no one's land. Virginia once had claim to what was nearly half the United States, but relinquished most of it to form new states. The Southerners fight for a dubious cause, but one must grant that they are fighting defensively, not in conquest."

"Then who were those people we have just seen run out of Peralta? What were they doing in New Mexico but trying to conquer it?"

"Those were Texans."

"Texans are Southerners. The armies that made war on us fifteen years ago were Southern. Your General Zachary Taylor, who became President Taylor, he was a Southerner. General Winfield Scott is from Virginia. Samuel Houston was a Virginian."

"Who stayed loyal to the Union."

"But when he fought against us, it was to bring slaves into Texas. Slavery was outlawed in Mexico when General Santa Ana was president. You Anglos wanted to change that—and you did. Slaves everywhere after Santa Ana was defeated."

"It may surprise you to learn that not all Southerners support that despicable institution. General Scott has been commander in chief of the Union armies, and whether all of them realize it or not, the end of slavery is what they are fighting for. I broke with my own family because they are slaveholders. My father will not speak to me because I detest slavery."

She smiled, competing with the sun. "Now I believe you when you say you are a Union man. I can see that now—in your face—the way you became angry with me for what I said."

"I mean no offense."

"My father is a Union man, too. He does not want New Mexico in the Confederacy. He is for Lincoln, and he is for Benito Juárez in Mexico. Those two words you said—those passwords—they are very appropriate."

"Your father is the man we are supposed to meet."

"Yes. He would have said 'Juárez' to your 'Lincoln' had he been in Peralta instead of me."

"Why didn't he come?"

"He stayed behind in Santa Fe to work for our cause. We will see him there."

"He will have information for me?"

"Oh yes. *Mucho.*"

He might yet contribute something to this mission. He could only wonder where Leahy might now be. Fort Union. Possibly Colorado.

As they rode on, he pondered her words. "You said 'our cause.' What did you mean by that?"

"The cause of freedom, Senor Raines. The cause of *libertad.*"

THEY sheltered for the night in a church at San Felipe Pueblo, a town inhabited mostly by Indians, from whom they were able to buy food. From that point, the trail veered away from the Rio Grande and led across barren desert to the highlands on which sat Santa Fe.

Tantou went off, without explanation or word of when he might return. Isabel, wrapped in her cloak, lay very close to Harry, lying on her back, gazing up at the darkened ceiling of the church.

"This is most improper, to be here like this with you," she said.

"You have nothing to fear."

"Before the war, it would have been improper for me to be seen alone with you on the plaza of Santa Fe. Now, so many things are done."

She turned onto her side, facing him, studying his face.

"You are a gentle man. Not much of a *pistolero*, though you pretend to be."

"I've killed two people in this war."

"Does it bother you?"

"Yes, it does."

"You see?" She leaned very close now, and then kissed him—softly, but for a very long time. Then she moved away, pulling her cloak about her again.

"That is all, Senor Raines. I know that you will not give me reason to regret that."

"No, but . . ."

"Good night."

A frustrating one. "Good night."

TANTOU returned before dawn and wakened them. They were into the Cerrillos Hills by afternoon. Clouds came and went over them, sparkling the landscape with brilliant moments of sunlight, then shrouding it in gloom.

Ascending a rise late in the day, they were able to glimpse Santa Fe in the distance. It seemed a magical, golden place in the glowing light of sunlight, a city in a fairy tale.

Harry hoped Isabel would be cheered by the sight, but her melancholy did not leave her. Then, all at once she smiled, spurring her horse.

There was a rider coming their way. As he drew nearer, Harry saw that it was a well-dressed Mexican, astride another magnificent horse. He was an older man, a trifle portly.

"Anselmo!" she cried.

Approaching Isabel, he removed his hat with a sweep.

"Senorita Almaden," he said, returning the sombrero to his head. "It is good to see you well. I was expecting not to find you for many days."

"Why are you trying to find me?" she asked. "You were asked to return home."

"And so I did, Isabelita." He looked away. There was something more he wanted to say.

Or did not want to.

The man glanced questioningly at Harry.

"This is the man we've been waiting for," she said. "A Union man, from the East."

Anselmo nodded, then turned his attention very directly to Isabel. "I have bad news. Very bad news."

"Something has gone wrong?" she asked.

"Your father is dead, Isabelita. He has been murdered."

Harry expected tears, a shriek, anger, or, as he might from the Southern ladies among whom he'd been brought up, fainting. Instead, her eyes went from the man Anselmo to the city waiting on the horizon. She furrowed her brow, then struck her horse with a vicious slap of reins to the flank and tore off down the road at a full, mad gallop.

Chapter 14

ONE-EYE was not a horse for sustained speed. As they fell farther and farther behind, Harry gave up and let the animal slow to a trot, with Tantou following suit. He reckoned it would not be hard to locate the Almaden family once he got to Santa Fe. He might well arrive an hour or more after her.

To his surprise, Anselmo, taking note of Harry's poor progress, slowed his own mount and at length fell in beside him.

"She will go to the house," Anselmo said.

"Her father was murdered?" Harry asked, as though he might have misunderstood.

"Yes," said the other, with a sigh. "A shotgun. It is well that it happened many days ago, and that he is now buried."

"Was it a robbery?"

A shrug. "Some things were missing, but, *quién sabe?*"

"You are a relative?"

"I work for the house of Don Luis Almaden. I am Anselmo Sabio. I manage the hacienda, and Don Luis's several businesses. I have been with them since Isabel was a *nena*."

"A what?"

"Baby."

"You said this happened many days ago. Why are you only now riding out to bring her the news?"

"There were many matters to attend to. We have been occupied by the enemy. They weren't proper soldiers. More a band of brigands. They called themselves that. I had much to do to protect Don Luis's holdings." He adjusted his hat. "And who are you, senor?"

Harry removed his own hat with a sweep. "Captain Harrison Raines, sir, a 'scout,' for want of a better term, for the United States Army—from Washington. I was to meet your Don Luis. Instead, in Peralta, there was Isabel—Senorita Almaden. We have escorted her from there. I and my friend here, Jack Tantou. He is also a scout."

Anselmo nodded to the Indian, who made no reply.

"I'm sorry for pestering you with so many questions," Harry said. "We came upon other murdered people on the trail. At one place, there was a man and a woman. Disturbing thing to see."

"And Isabel saw this?"

"No. This was before we met. Farther down the Rio Grande. I came up from El Paso."

"Where is the Confederate Army now?" Anselmo asked.

"Pretty far south of Peralta, I'd say, and riding hard to get farther. There was a battle of sorts at Peralta. It was mostly artillery—very little small arms combat. No one really won the fight, but the Rebels moved out fast after it was over. I think they are going back to Texas. They had no supply wagons."

"I hope they suffer much on that trail. They are the nastiest soldiers I ever did see. No one in what you call the Mexican War behaved so badly toward us. I think we in Santa Fe would rather have had to deal with Apache or Commanche than those Texans."

"Who killed Isabel's father?"

Anselmo shook his head sadly. "We do not know. There are suspicions, but . . . It happened as the Confederates were pulling out. Don Luis was alone in his study. There was much looting and pillaging in the town. Maybe it was a Confederate straggler. Maybe one of Don Luis's enemies in Santa Fe. He had some. Don Luis was a very political person. A reformer. They make many enemies."

Harry wished he knew this man better. He found himself liking him, but, in this country, that could prove folly.

"I was to meet with Senor Almaden," Harry said. "He was, I gather, a friend to the Union cause. I would like to help you in this, if I may. Whatever I can do."

"There is no need, senor. This family has friends. Don Luis has two sons. And . . ."

Harry waited. When the man still did not continue, he spoke up himself.

"Two sons, you said?"

"Roberto and Eduardo. I think they may be with the Union Army. They have not yet come home."

"As I say, I would be happy to help."

"*Capitán*, I know that Isabel is a very beautiful girl. *Mucho encantador*."

"That's not why," Harry said, less than truthfully, and not knowing what *encantador* meant. "Senor Almaden was an important friend to the Union out here. If the Confederates were in any way responsible for his death, they will want to know that back in Washington."

Pinkerton would want to know. The rule for the Secret Service was an eye for an eye. Spies on both sides usually claimed to be military scouts when captured, and were thus held as prisoners of war and ultimately exchanged. If Harry found himself compelled to identify himself as anything out here, it was as a scout, for this most compelling of reasons. But if the South were to commence murdering the other side's agents, it would require a reply in kind. Pinkerton had a dozen or more Rebel agents imprisoned at Fort McHenry he'd be willing to bring to the gallows in retaliation—more at Fort Delaware. He had a long list of Confederate agents still at large in Washington City, half of them living in the National Hotel.

"Washington is a long way from Santa Fe, senor. I am sure the interest there in occurrences here is very small."

"If it were small, sir, I and my associates would not be here. The Union Army would not be here. I am obligated to Senorita Almaden. I believe our lives were saved at her intercession. I intend to assist her in this if I can."

"*Capitán.* We want no more trouble. There has been too much of that. This is a family matter. Believe me, no good will come of it if you intrude. It will not please Isabel."

"I have business in Santa Fe. I will be staying there several days in any case."

"Suit yourself, *Capitán.* It is a pleasant place." He gave Harry a deferential nod then spurred his horse into a canter.

Harry and Tantou kept theirs to a walk, watching Anselmo's lengthening trail of dust.

"What do you think, Jack?"

"I think she is beautiful, like he says."

"That's not why I want to stay."

"You are a poor liar—for a 'scout.' "

"Well, you are right. She is why. But I should be very curious about her father's death no matter what."

"Why is that, Harry Raines?"

"I am curious to know why that man doesn't want our help."

The creases in Tantou's face deepened into a grin. "Maybe he thinks our help won't help."

Harry kicked One-Eye into a trot.

UNION troops—at least two companies, perhaps more— had taken possession of Santa Fe and were using the Palace of Governors and a small redoubt called Fort Marcy as headquarters. The American flag was flying above the Palace and infantry were posted all along it. Harry trotted by, eyes forward, not wanting any business with them yet.

There was a hotel on the other side of the plaza. Pulling up before a hitching rail, Harry remained in the saddle until Tantou had come up beside him.

"You'll be wanting to rejoin your unit?" Harry said.

Tantou shook his head. "They are far away from here."

Harry pointed across the square. "One block."

"I was scout for General Carleton. He came out of California with more than two thousand men, but spent more time fighting Indians than Rebels. Chiricahua Apaches led by Mangas Coloradas and Cochise. Very big chiefs. *Tres mechant*. Not what I signed up for. They give Carleton a very hard time. I do not think he has reached Tucson yet. I left him and came east."

"Are you a deserter?"

"I signed up to lead him east. It is not my fault he did not come with me."

Harry dismounted. It felt wonderful to escape the saddle and flex his knees. He wrapped his reins around the rail, dusted off his coat and vest, then turned to see what Tantou was going to do.

The Meti just sat there, waiting.

"Do you want to stay with me?" Harry asked.

"You are truly a government man? From Washington?"

"Don't voice that about too much, but, yes. I have not been lying to you."

"I may need your protection."

"As I have needed yours."

"And you will go north soon? To Colorado?"

"If that's the nearest telegraph, yes. But maybe not soon."

Tantou closed his eyes, as though taking advice from inner voices. Then, finally, he dismounted. "Yes. I will stay with you."

Paying an exorbitant sum, Harry was able to procure a small room overlooking the plaza. The sum was sufficiently great for the desk clerk to pay no attention when Tantou accompanied him upstairs.

HAVING left the Meti to clean and load their weapons and find a stable for their horses, Harry set out upon the town on foot, intent on making significant improvements of his person. This involved a hot bath, a shave and moustache trim, a haircut, and two new suits, both black. He also bought four shirts and replaced his hat and boots.

His old clothes were so stiff with old sweat and dirt they could almost stand by themselves. Returning to the hotel, he offered them to Tantou, who declined. Harry gave them to the hotel's elderly Mexican porter.

There was a cantina at one end of the plaza. Harry wasn't certain he'd be welcome there and was pretty sure there'd be no card game. He started across the square in the opposite direction, thinking he might look for an Anglo saloon with better prospects for convivial gambling.

Something drew his attention to the Palace of the Governors. It was a sand-colored horse, being held by a cavalry trooper standing near the long building's main door. Harry had not noticed it before, having kept his eyes averted when he rode past.

He came nearer. The saddle was different—military, with high pommel and cantle. But it was the same animal. There was no mistaking it.

"Excuse me, soldier," he said, approaching. "Where did you get that horse?"

"U.S. Army property."

"But I know that animal. It belongs to someone else."

"Used to. Mexican named Don Carlos or some such. But he's dead."

"No. I talking about an Irishman. His name's Leahy. This is his horse."

"No it ain't. And it wasn't. Provost marshal's got him locked up."

"I'm talking about a man named Joseph Leahy."

"Right. That's him. Horse thief. They got him locked up, and there's gonna be a hanging."

Chapter 15

THE Union officer set the small piece of paper Harry had given him carefully on the desktop before him, smoothed it out, and leaned close to read it. He wrinkled his nose, frowning.

"I've been carrying it hidden in my boot," said Harry. "Sorry."

"Got worse smells 'n that in this army," said the officer, a captain named Hosfeldt. "What bothers me is what in hell you think you're proving by showing me this."

"It's a pass—through any Union line—signed by President Lincoln himself."

"You say that's what it is, but how do I know that for certain? I have never seen Mr. Lincoln write his name—or anything that was claimed to be his writing. Maybe you wrote this."

Harry had carried the pass all the way from Washington, knowing it could mean his life if it was found on him by the wrong people, but that it might possibly save his life as well. Now it seemed as good as worthless.

"I did not write his name, sir. I believe that forging the signature of the president of the United States is a capital crime."

He had no idea if this was true, but he hoped it sounded persuasive.

"Maybe it is real, but it doesn't say you are what you say."

"Captain, the federal government would have little use for a spy who wandered about the Confederacy carrying a paper that said 'I am a Union spy.' I am sorry but this is the best I can do. If we were within reach of a telegraph, I'd send to Washington for bonafides. But we are weeks away from one, and my colleague, Mr. Leahy, cannot wait that long, can he?"

"You say Senorita Almaden will vouch for you?"

"Yes, sir. She rescued me from a gang of Rebel soldiers in Peralta. Broke me out of their jail. I think I owe her my life. But I am uncertain as to her disposition at the moment. Her father's death has grievously disturbed her."

"It disturbed us all. He was one of the heroes at Glorieta."

Harry gave him a blank look. He heard about the Union victory in the pass but had no notion of how it was won.

"He and Colonel Manuel Chavez of the New Mexico volunteers led Major Chivington and his men over the mesa. They hit the Rebel base at the head of the canyon and burned all their supply wagons. Bastards had no choice but to pull out and run for Texas."

"I know. We were still in Peralta when they came through."

"The Spanish people here took Don Luis's murder hard. Same with Don Carlos Martinez y Lomas getting killed down south. Which is why this man Joseph Leahy is at risk for his neck."

"I thought he was accused of stealing a horse."

"That horse outside, he belonged to Don Carlos. Your man Leahy came riding in on him. Somebody recognized the animal. When he said the owner was dead, the locals were ready to string him up right then and there. Our provost marshal intervened and locked him up, as much for the man's own safety as anything. But the local sheriff'll be back tomorrow, and it's likely he'll move things along smartly. Your man could be a-dangle by tomorrow sundown."

"And if you discover you've hanged an agent of the U.S. Secret Service? One who has been in the personal service of President Lincoln and helped him evade an assassination plot by a Secesh gang in Baltimore?"

Hosfeldt fidgeted. "It's the townspeople and the local law. Not us."

"I was with Leahy when we came upon the man who had this horse. He said his name was San Jeronimo," Harry continued. "He died a few minutes later—shot through the back. Never said a word. We buried him as best we could."

"San Jeronimo? That makes no sense. This horse belonged to Don Carlos Martinez."

"Well, whoever the animal belongs to, Leahy took it only because we had news to bring to you people about the Rebels being on the march. His own beat-up mount wouldn't have lasted a mile. I'll testify to this."

"You mean to identify yourself and Leahy in open court as Union spies?"

Harry rubbed his chin. "Why can't he remain in military custody? You are the authority here. I told you. We're federal agents. Good God, sir. You can't let this happen."

"My colonel's the authority here."

"And where is he?"

"Up at the Santa Clara Pueblo. Meeting with Indians. The Rebels got them all stirred up."

"When does he come back?"

The captain shrugged.

"I'd like to see Mr. Leahy."

"Sure. Can't think of the harm in that."

THEY had put Leahy in a stable, along with a dozen or more Confederate officers and soldiers who'd been captured lingering too long in the town. The Irishman was sitting with a Rebel sergeant. He looked up when Harry and the Union captain entered, but finished his conversation before rising. He walked with an odd twist to the swing of his leg.

"Did they shoot you?" Harry asked.

"That splendid animal, as you called him, threw me twice," Leahy replied.

"Threw you, or let you fall off?"

"The result's the same, boyo."

"He has got you in some considerable trouble, I see."

"Nothing at all to worry about." He looked over his shoulder at his fellow prisoners, then to Captain Hosfeldt. "Would there be a place more private where my friend and I can talk, sir?"

The captain nodded toward the door. "You can go out in the corral, but I'll have to go with you. And if you try to run for it, I'll have to shoot you—if one of the locals don't do it for me."

They followed the officer out into the bright sunlight. There were two privates with muskets leaning against the fence. Hosfeldt went over to them, leaving Harry and Leahy to their business. He lighted a cigar, eyeing them a little worriedly through the first puff of smoke.

Harry drew Leahy to the other side of the corral. "For a former police detective, you do spend a considerable amount of time in jail."

"All for the good cause, Raines."

"You're in serious risk of a rope this time, Joseph. It's not a matter to take lightly."

Leahy's bright blue eyes seemed almost mirthful. "I am in no risk of a rope. Certainly not about to be hanged by the very army we're in the service of. Mr. Pinkerton wouldn't have it."

"Mr. Pinkerton isn't here. The plan is to leave it up to the local law. The Mexican community is unhappy and riled up. They think you killed the man we found—who the army says was a Don Carlos Martinez. They know you came in on his horse. And there's talk you may also have murdered one of the local heroes. A Don Luis Almaden y Cortes. He helped the Union boys win their battle here. The town sees him as a savior—and a martyr."

"I know all about that. I know all about a lot of things. These Rebels are talkative fellows. All the more so, as they managed to bring some whiskey in here with them. You know that I disapprove of spiritous liquors, but they worked their evil to good effect for our cause. I've learned much, Harry. That's why I allowed myself to be imprisoned here, and why I remain."

"What can they possibly have to say that's any use now? You rode off to warn the Union commander the Rebels were heading north, and I'm betting you got there after the battle that sent them running south again."

"That is the case, aye. But I've learned a lot nevertheless. Names of those here who are loyal and names of those who not. Plots afoot. The damned Rebels are turning every Indian tribe they can against Federal authority—and there are Mexicans longing for the good old days of Santa Ana, and seeing a main chance here."

"They're probably the ones readying the hemp for you."

"Fear not. I have made inquires about the local judge."

"What do you mean? Are you thinking of bribing him?"

"No need, laddy buck. No need of that."

Harry took note of several Mexicans gathered on the street opposite. "What can I do for you now, Joseph?"

"The grub's all right. Certainly I have no use for liquor or tobacco. Perhaps, if you have a convenient moment, you might find out who did shoot this Don Carlos."

"So, you are worried, after all."

"Not worried, boyo. Just curious." He leaned close. "Do you still have that sack of gold coins we found?"

"Yes, though it's an amazement that I do."

"Where is it?"

"In my hotel room."

Leahy shook his head. "If, sir, you might find a somewhat safer place for its keeping, you might then get the word out that I took it and hid it somewhere. Maybe then the interest in my hasty demise will abate."

"I'll ask Tantou to scout one out."

"And who in blazes is Tantou?"

"Jack Tantou. He's an Indian scout—half Indian, actually. The other half's French Canadian."

"What's a Canadian doing way down here?"

"Working for the army. At least, he was."

"Which army?"

"Ours, of course."

"You trust him?"

"He saved my life, when he certainly didn't have to. I was ambushed by Indians. Apaches."

"Not exactly Virginia, is it now?"

"Strangest place I've ever been to."

The Irishman returned the stares of the Mexicans across the street.

"It may be, Harry, that we will ultimately have to devise some means of escape. Just in case."

JACK Tantou had anticipated Harry's need. He had buried the bag of gold and the other items they'd taken from the Rio Grande dead in the churchyard of the Mission of San Miguel, not far.

"How did you manage that in bright daylight?"

"I went to the mission wall there and sat for a very long time, digging while I did."

The hotel room they were sharing had but one chair, and Tantou was in it. Harry went to the bed. His body was screaming for sleep.

He sat down. "Jack, would you mind pretending for a bit to be my servant?"

Tantou thought a moment, then shrugged. "How long is a 'bit'?"

"A few days. Just till we're quit of this place."

"I will pretend. But I will not empty your chamber pot."

Harry smiled and leaned back onto the mattress. "Certainly not. What I need for you to do is mingle with some of the real servants in this town. I want them to hear from you that there was a bag of gold with Don Carlos Martinez but that Joseph Leahy took it and hid it somewhere."

"Not the San Miguel church."

"No. Tell them you don't know where, but you'd like to."

Tantou stood quietly, then grunted, and left the room without another word.

Harry slept. When he awoke to the wind rattling the shutters, it occurred to him it might be useful now to visit the cantina on the plaza. He had small knowledge of Spanish, but perhaps the locals had made some accommodation to being part of the United States, however unwillingly.

He went directly there and asked for whiskey. The barkeep frowned and shook his head, putting down a bottle of tequila in lieu. Harry nodded reluctant approval.

The taste was oddly sweet. After a second sip, he turned his back to the bar to survey the room. Instead of being observed, he found himself completely ignored, as though deliberately. Shunned. By the time he'd finished his glass and poured another, no one had come near him. And then someone did.

It was the man Anselmo. He entered in some haste, went straight to the bar, took note of Harry, and then moved down to him.

"*Buenos días*, senor," he said.

"Good afternoon, sir. May I offer you a dram?"

"A dram?"

"A drink."

"*Sí. Muchas gracias.*"

They both drank. Anselmo savored his. He struck Harry as a man who was serious about most everything, including pleasures.

"How is the beautiful Senorita Almaden?"

"Still beautiful. Still sad."

"I should like to speak to her."

Anselmo sipped again of the tequila, then shook his head slowly, as though his response had come from some deep well of wisdom. "Not now."

"I would like to visit the house of Don Carlos Martinez then."

"It is too sad a household for such a visit now."

"Anselmo. Two men are dead. A friend of mine is being held on suspicion of killing one of them. But I know next to nothing about either man."

"The Martinez house is in mourning."

"I will be sensitive to their bereavement. We are taught proper deportment where I come from."

"And where is that?"

"Virginia. I am what they call a Virginia gentleman. It's not a description. It is a birthright. Like being a don out here."

Two men rose from their table and came to the bar, standing near Anselmo and Harry. They were well dressed and middle aged. Either could have been the late Don Luis, as Harry imagined him.

"I still fear you would be intruding, senor," Anselmo said, nodding to the two men as they looked his way.

"Who is there in his family?"

"A wife. A son named Alejandro. But he has been gone for many weeks. To Mexico. The war may be preventing him from returning."

Harry had fixed his mind on the image of the dying man holding the reins of the magnificent horse. "How old is this Alejandro?"

"He is grown. Twenty-four, twenty-five years old."

"And Don Carlos Martinez?"

"He is Alejandro's father. He fought along with Don Luis in the war with the United States. He was at Taos."

"What happened at Taos?"

"There was a revolt against the U.S. occupiers of the Mexican land. The governor was killed. Many Mexicans were killed by the time it was over. Indians, too."

Harry finished his drink. "I am going to the Martinez house. Will you tell me where it is?"

The other pursed his lips. He was very clean shaven, unlike most in this town.

"Do you want to learn who killed Don Luis?" Harry asked, having received no reply to his other question.

"*Sí*. Of course."

"Then let us go."

An old woman answered the door—a servant, but obviously one in much authority.

"I would like to speak to Senora Martinez, *por favor*." Harry had been picking up bits of Spanish.

"Is not here." She looked to Anselmo and spoke to him rapidly in Spanish.

He frowned, shaking his head.

"What did she say?" Harry asked.

"She said Don Carlos's wife went south with him—down the Rio Grande."

"South?"

"*Sí.*"

Harry had been brought up according to the dictum that a gentleman never insults—unless he does so deliberately. He needed to commit a serious breach of manners, and did so—deliberately—moving past the woman and entering the house. Anselmo remained on the doorstep.

"Has Alejandro come home?" Harry asked.

The woman looked from him to Anselmo and back again. Anselmo spoke in rapid Spanish again, receiving a voluble response. Now, Anselmo stepped inside.

"Alejandro has not returned," he said to Harry. "This is Maria Gonzales—the housekeeper. She has not heard from any of the Martinezes, and she is worried."

Harry glanced down the hall. There were doors to left and right, both open. "I fear she has reason to be."

"She has no money."

Harry thought of the gold coins Tantou had hidden. "There may be something we can do about that. Tell her."

Anselmo did so, then looked to Harry, as if wondering what was coming next.

"Is this the parlor?" he asked, indicating the wide wooden door to the right.

"*Sí.*"

"Excuse me," Harry said, with a bow to the housekeeper. Then he moved quickly to the door and stepped into the room beyond.

As he hoped, there were several glass plate photographs on the mantel, set in velvet boxed frames. He pointed to them. "Don Carlos?"

The woman's face went blank, then showed a spark of comprehension. "*Sí*, senor." She went to the mantel and pointed to the photograph in the center.

Harry went up to it, prompting her to back away. Holding the image toward the window light, he examined it closely. It was a formal portrait of a well-to-do Mexican couple—the man seated, the woman standing to the side and slightly behind. They were middle-aged. She was slightly plump, but still unusually attractive, with large dark eyes. He had a wide moustache.

"The man we came upon," Harry said to Anselmo. "The one with the horse, the one who died and we buried beneath rocks. This is not him. If this man in the picture is Don Carlos, then the dead man with the sand-colored horse is not him."

"Don Carlos could be alive then?" Anselmo asked.

Harry leaned closer, finding his spectacles and putting them in place. "This is Senora Martinez?"

"*Sí. Cierto.*"

He had no real idea what the couple in the horseless buckboard might have looked like, but he recognized the dress. It was the same as that worn by the woman in the photograph.

"I do not think they are alive," Harry said.

HARRY gave the woman a five dollar coin and then departed. He wanted to look through the house more thoroughly, and there would doubtless be more to ask of her, but the questions weren't clearly drawn in his mind as yet.

Anselmo caught up with him at the corner, moving out of the way as a squadron of Union cavalry trotted by.

"What are you thinking, Senor Raines?"

"I am thinking my friend Leahy is being held for the wrong murder. The man we found and buried is not your Don Carlos. I can only wonder how he came by that horse. He may well have been Don Carlos's murderer."

"I don't understand."

Harry started walking down the street. "I'm going back to the plaza. May I buy you another drink?"

"I will walk with you to the plaza, but I have no interest in more to drink."

"Come to think of it, I don't either."

"You said you thought Don Carlos and his wife were dead. How do you know this?"

"After we encountered the dying man who had Don Carlos's horse—several days later, farther up the Rio Grande—I came upon a dead man and woman. They'd been shot. Buzzards or vultures had picked over their faces, so there would be no telling who they were to look at them. But the woman was wearing the same dress that I saw in the photograph on the mantel. It is my presumption that they were Senor and Senora Martinez."

"They were richly dressed?"

"Yes."

"And did you bury them, too?"

"Yes. More thoroughly than we did that other poor devil."

"And did you retain any of their possessions? To return to kin?"

The right lie was needed here. "Yes. But I'm afraid they got left behind in Peralta. All that shooting, you know."

"But you're sure it was the same dress?"

"Oh indeed, sir. I could not possibly forget it." He fumbled in his pocket, retrieving a small piece of jewelry. "And she was wearing this brooch."

Anselmo nodded thoughtfully. "I have seen this on her. This is a very complicated matter."

A shopkeeper was closing the doors and shutters of his store across the way. Harry could not make out for certain what his wares were.

"I would like very much to call upon Senorita Almaden," he said.

"So you have said several times."

"I would like to call upon her tomorrow, if convenient."

"I will inquire. If she assents, I will have word sent to your hotel."

"Thank you."

They walked on, pausing at a side street as a small funeral procession emerged from it—a young priest leading a bent, slow-moving old man—the apparent bereaved.

"His wife, poor lady," said Anselmo. "The brigands. She died of the fright."

"New Mexico is well rid of the Confederates. They are better people in their own country, I suppose."

Anselmo seemed puzzled at this. "But your government claims it all as one country. That is why you are fighting this unhappy war."

"We are fighting this war to end Negro servitude. When that is done, the rest of it will follow."

"I don't understand."

"It's a common complaint." They were at the plaza. Harry turned to face Anselmo. "I was going to ask you— how did you and Senorita Almaden get to Peralta?"

"What do you mean?"

"What transport?"

"On horseback. As you saw."

TANTOU, sitting cross-legged in a corner of the room, was feeling grumbly, having been turned away from the hotel's restaurant.

"They must expect me to go out into the desert and kill coyotes for food," he said. "Have you ever tasted coyote?"

"They are a backward people out here," Harry said, collapsing into the room's only chair. "But it might help if you weren't dressed like someone out of *The Last of the Mohicans*."

Tantou grunted. "That is a stupid book."

Harry didn't know whether his friend was speaking from the Huron or French Canadian point of view. He did not pursue the criticism, with which he wholly agreed.

"Our mystery has deepened," he said. "I went to the house of this man Don Carlos Martinez and saw a photograph of him and his wife. I believe they are one and the same as the couple we found in the buckboard."

"Two and the same."

"That was his sand-colored horse that Leahy and I found with the dying man I thought was Don Carlos. The dying man must have stolen it. He may have killed Don Carlos and his wife in the process."

"An Indian might, but a white man would not kill people like that for a horse."

"You forget the thousand dollars in gold."

"True, white men kill all the time for just that."

"But who shot him?"

Tantou shut his eyes. "Let us go to Denver."

"I thought you were hungry. I'm sure they will serve you in the cantina across the plaza."

"Okay. We eat before we go to Denver."

THE main room was crowded, but they were able to obtain a table in the corner farthest from the fire. As before, Harry found many eyes upon him. The two gentlemen who had stood at the bar near him and Anselmo were not present.

A serving girl came to their table with a jug of beer that proved warmer than the room. Tantou ordered venison and beans; Harry, a beefsteak and beans. She possessed little English, but seemed to understand him.

"Has Alejandro Martinez been in recently?" Harry asked.

Her expression remained blank.

"Alejandro Martinez? The son of Don Carlos Martinez?"

She turned away and went to the kitchen. She was barefoot, and there was a flash of ankle.

"You worry about the wrong murder, Harry Raines," Tantou said.

"Which one should I be worrying about—in this town, with such an abundance of them?"

"You should worry about the one that Isabel Almaden worries about."

"She may grant me an audience tomorrow. But I must get Leahy out of jail."

Tantou grunted. Their food came, steaming hot. They ate every crumb and scrap and drank all the beer.

When they returned to the street, it was fully dark. Tantou took a step toward the plaza, but Harry held him back. He was feeling warm and happy from his meal. And perhaps too bold.

"I want to go back to the Martinez house," he said.

"Why?"

"I want to see what goes on there at night when they are not expecting company."

"Not much. Everyone there is dead."

"Let's take a look."

*   *   *

THE side gate to the courtyard was locked, but, looking over the wall, they could see lights in the upstairs window of the house. Harry drew into the shadows and kept watch a moment. As he stood there, he found he could hear voices with some clarity. One was a woman's, the other a young man's. He could not follow the Spanish, but the subject was serious, and the exchange of words strong.

Tantou's hand gripped his shoulder tightly. "Run, Harry Raines. Run fast."

Harry tried to look around to see what in blazes the Indian was talking about, but something heavy hit the top of his head before he could manage an inch.

Chapter 16

HARRY regained consciousness but remained in blackness. He tried to touch his injured crown, but his hands were bound at the wrist. Shaking his head slightly, he discovered it was covered with some sort of hood. He was swaying, which he at first thought was due to dizziness, but realized he was aboard some sort of conveyance, quite probably a coach. Judging by the relative comfort of the ride and the plush of the seat, he guessed it was a well-made and expensive one. His assailants—and he heard several voices now—were not mere street thugs.

"Where are you taking me?" he said.

The voices stopped.

"Who are you? Where are you taking me?"

The reply was a cuff to his right ear. He kept silent thereafter.

HE could sense when the carriage made a turn. As these became more frequent, and his seat assumed a tilt, it was clear they were following an ascending road. Harry wasn't certain of the direction in which they were traveling, but presumed they were climbing the foothills of the Sangre de Cristo range. The mountains to the west of Santa Fe were too far away.

After a while, the voices resumed. They spoke in Spanish, apparently safe in the knowledge that he did not much understand the tongue. The only ones who were aware of that fact were Tantou, Anselmo, and the beautiful Isabel.

Once in the hills, they were a long time getting to their destination, following a road that became progressively bumpier. When they arrived, Harry stumbled while descending from the coach. No one attempted to break his fall but several hands reached for him after he hit the ground—all pulling him swiftly to his feet.

"This way," said someone in English, jerking him forward. The voice was accented, Mexican.

"Gracias," said Harry.

The night air at this elevation was cold, but the interior of the house or building they'd brought him to was quite warm. They thrust him down into a chair, leaning over his shoulder to untie his hands, only to bind them individually to the arms of the chair. A moment later, the hood was swept from his head and, blinking, he found himself staring into the high flames of a blazing fire.

"Do not look behind you," the Mexican-accented voice said. "You will regret it."

"Gracias," said Harry. "I surely won't."

In the glare of flame, he could see little, but in time it occurred to him that a man had taken a chair beside his, and was staring intently at him. A quick side glance showed Harry two large dark eyes above a black bandana wound around most of the face. It also showed the twin barrels of a shotgun, staring at him just as intently.

"Who are you?" the man asked.

"Harrison Raines, sir. Of Charles City County, Virginia. The Belle Haven plantation. Also Washington City, and more recently, the Confederate capital at Richmond."

"How can you be from both capitals?"

"I have lived in both places. And I carry passes through the lines."

"How is that?"

"I'm a civilian. I trade in horses. I sell to both sides."

There was some discussion behind him, in Spanish. When it concluded, the questioning resumed.

"And on what side are you?"

Harry had to make a quick calculation. These people had obviously been aware of his presence in Santa Fe for some time. He had come to the town after the Confederates had fled it. He had gone to the Palace of Governors and talked with a Union officer, and had settled into his hotel for a stay of some days. It would be safe to presume that his loyalty lay with the Federals.

So, if these people were as loyal to the side of Lincoln, there would be no need of this secrecy. Santa Fe was again Union territory—probably for good. They could have approached him openly—certainly without need of this clandestine nocturnal journey into the wilds. The likely presumption was that they were Rebel agents, an underground of sorts—or at the least people who had common cause with the Confederacy.

Yet most of the Mexican population had fought with the Union side in territorial militias. Two of them, Lieu-

tenant Colonel Chavez and Isabel's dead father, had made
Union victory possible.

He had to make a draw—as with cards. "My father and
brother are officers in the Confederate cavalry," he said,
finally. "I am a Virginian. I am useful to my state in my
own way."

His eyes went fully now to the twin shotgun barrels.
These people could indeed be vigilantes of some sort, bent
on punishing Confederate sympathizers for the deprivations
of the Texas "brigands." Punishing them without recourse
to cumbersome courts or military tribunals. Punishing
them swiftly, as with a quick pull of shotgun triggers.

"You have proof of this?"

"*Sí*. I have a letter signed by General Robert E. Lee
himself."

"Who is General Lee?"

"He is President Jefferson Davis's principal general."

"Show me this letter."

"I cannot, unless you untie my hands."

Someone who'd apparently been standing just behind
him reached over and undid the rope that held Harry's
right hand fast to his chair. The left remained bound.

With difficulty, Harry retrieved the letter from the hiding place he'd fashioned within the cuff of his coat. He
shook the paper into its full length and handed it over.
More of the ink had been blurred in travel, but the reference at the top to the Confederate States Navy and General
Lee's signature written boldly at the bottom were both still
clearly legible.

The man with the shotgun leaned close to the fire to
read it. Harry gathered he was as near of sight as himself.

"Satisfied?" Harry asked, when the man was done.

"Satisfied? No, senor. Only more curious." He refolded

the letter and gave it back to Harry—a good sign. Now he brought the shotgun to bear again. Not a good sign. "Tell us, please, why you have come to Santa Fe. And do not say it was to trade horses."

He had told Isabel the truth, that he was working for the Union, and that he was going to the territorial capital to find the Federal army. These men, then, had not communicated with her. If they had talked to Anselmo, she had apparently not discussed it with him either.

"A friend of mine is being wrongfully held for the murder of one of your local citizens." Harry related the rest of the strange tale of the dying man with the sand-colored horse and the later encounter with the couple in the buckboard. He refrained from revealing his discovery that the man and woman were likely Don Carlos Martinez and his wife. That was knowledge quite possibly dangerous to have, which might excite their curiosity about him in unpleasant ways.

"Who is this Indian who was with you?"

"Half Indian. A Union army scout lately out of California. The vanguard of what might be a large federal force."

"He's a strange traveling companion for a friend of this General Lee."

"Strange, perhaps. But a useful one."

"Where is he?"

"I've no idea. He comes and goes as he will."

There was further discussion among the people behind him in Spanish.

"If we let you go, you must say nothing about this encounter to anyone—Union or Confederate—*comprende?* To do so will be to invite a bad end for you."

"Certainly not. I will put any such notion from my

mind." Lest he have nightmares about the wide variety of bad ends doubtless available to these people.

"But we may want further conversation with you."

Harry rubbed the top of his head with his free hand. "No need to announce yourselves in this forceful fashion."

"If you contrive to free your friend from jail—or if he goes to the gallows—will you then leave town?"

Harry didn't want to answer that until he had talked with Isabel. "If that is everyone's pleasure. Though it is very nice here."

More talk in Spanish. Then suddenly the hood was returned to his head.

INSTEAD of bringing him back to town, they dumped him out of the coach onto the side of a country road. They had loosened his bonds, but by the time he got his hands free and the hood removed, they had passed from view, though he could hear the sound of their carriage and accompanying outriders as they rode into the distance. Having been under the hood, he could see clearly in the starlight, but had no notion of direction. He had spent much of his youth sailing in boats on the James, but there'd been little need for knowing celestial navigation on the river.

He deduced the best way to go would be the same way taken by his erstwhile captors and commenced a trudge in that direction along the hard, rocky track.

He had progressed not fifty yards when he heard hoofbeats coming up behind him. His hosts had given him back his weapons, but he had no time to bring up either Navy Colt or derringer by the time the rider was upon him.

There was no need. "You okay, Harry Raines?" said Tantou.

"Yes. Where in blazes have you been?"

"When they took you, I followed. It's been a long ride."

"You know where we are?"

"Some miles to the north of Santa Fe—in foothills of the Sangre de Cristo." He extended his hand, to pull Harry up onto the horse behind him. It took a second try.

Harry was glad to be there, despite the discomfort. "We'll have to go back at a walk," Harry said.

"Be thankful you are going back." The horse began its plod.

"Could you find this place again?"

"I can find any place again."

When they reached the outskirts of Santa Fe, Tantou made him dismount, then did so himself. He looked around carefully and smacked the animal on the hindquarters. It broke into a trot, heading straight for the town.

"What did you do that for?" Harry asked.

"It is not my horse. I did not have time to fetch and saddle mine if I was to follow you. So I stole someone else's."

Chapter 17

THERE was a café two streets over from the plaza where tables had been set up in the courtyard beneath a warming morning sun. Harry and Tantou were there as soon as it opened for breakfast, ordering beefsteak, eggs, and coffee. No one objected to Tantou's presence, though the waiter looked askance at the Meti's practice of holding his meat in his left hand, while cutting chewable pieces from it with a Bowie knife wielded by his right.

"How are you this morning, Harry Raines?" he asked, between chews.

"My head hurts as though from strong drink, though I had but little."

"The remedy is the same for both."

"It's too early," Harry said. "Though I am tempted."

The Indian looked to the sky. "A fine day to begin a journey."

"Leahy first. Then journey. We will all go to Denver together."

"Unless he hangs."

"Please, Jack."

"Some men are born to hang. It is in their nature. Like the ways of the animals of the forest. The rabbit is born to be eaten."

"He is not going to hang. Joseph Leahy is no rabbit."

At first they had been the only customers in the court-yard. Now they were not. Anselmo stood in the arched doorway leading to the street. He observed Harry and Tan-tou a while, as though waiting for them to do something. When Harry waved, he came forth.

"How did you know we were here?"

"By looking for you," Anselmo said. "This is the fourth place I've been to this morning."

Harry gestured to a chair, but the Mexican remained standing. Tantou continued eating.

"How may we be of assistance to you, sir?" Harry asked.

"It is I who am being of assistance to you."

Tantou stopped eating, and waited.

"How so?"

"Senorita Almaden will see you."

"When?"

"Now, if you please."

Tantou resumed eating.

"I won't be but a moment," Harry said to Anselmo.

ISABEL received him in the parlor of her father's house. She wore a black mourning dress so elegant that, with more décolletage, it might have been a ball gown. She offered her hand. Uncertain as to the custom but very happy to see her, Harry kissed it. She did not object.

"Where is your friend?" she asked.

"Jack Tantou? He is finishing his breakfast. Actually, I think by now he must be finishing my breakfast."

"I did not mean to take you from it."

He smiled, hoping that would not be unseemly, given her somber, mourning mood. "It was I who asked to see you, Isabel. I am grateful for the opportunity to do so. The loss you have suffered with the death of your father grieves me greatly. I am told the Union had no greater friend in New Mexico.

Her dark eyes grew more so. "He was a good man. A good father. This has nothing to do with Union or Confederacy."

"I'm sorry."

Isabel retreated to a high-backed wooden chair that much resembled a throne. She seated herself and beckoned him to a smaller, simpler chair near it.

"What do you know of my father's death?" she asked, after waiting for Anselmo to leave the room. "What do the Federal soldiers say?"

"I know nothing beyond what Anselmo has told me, which is that it was murder. The Federal officer I talked to said your father's passing was a loss to the Union and the cause of great unhappiness in the Spanish community. But there is more concern now about the death of Don Carlos Martinez and his wife."

"And why is that?"

"I don't know. Perhaps because they have arrested someone they have accused of doing it."

"A friend of yours named Leahy."

"You are well informed."

"Santa Fe is a small place, Harry. There is to be a court hearing this afternoon. Judge Ambrose has returned, as has

Sheriff Oates." She drew one finger across the corner of her right eye. "Some say he could have killed my father, this friend of yours. He is your friend, yes—this man they have?"

"He could not have done it. He arrived in Santa Fe after your father was murdered."

"One can be in Santa Fe without arriving. Then slip away and 'arrive' later." A small smile came to her lips, bringing memories of that desert night.

"The dead man Leahy took the horse from was not Don Carlos Martinez. We don't know who he was, but Martinez and his wife were killed elsewhere, and at a different time."

She shuddered as Harry began to describe the scene at the horseless wagon in full detail, identifying the victims.

"No more," she said, cutting him short with a wave of her hand. "I do not want to hear about Don Carlos."

"Were not he and your father friends?"

They were interrupted by the entrance of Anselmo, bearing a tray with two stone mugs of coffee. He served them and then remained standing, as though to be of assistance to Isabel.

"I will be here some days," Harry said, after taking a steamy sip. "I have offered my assistance as concerns your father."

The smile vanished. "Offered it to whom?"

"To me, Senorita," said Anselmo. "I told him this is a matter for our community to settle."

Anselmo had done an excellent job with this coffee. Harry regretted having to leave his unfinished. He stood up. "Very well, Isabel. I am glad to see that you returned home safely. I will not bother you further."

He gave her a small nod of a bow, then strode toward the door.

"How can you help?" she said. Implicit in her tone was doubt, borne, Harry assumed, of the not entirely competent manner in which he had dealt with the Confederates in Peralta.

"I don't know yet, but I will do as much as I possibly can."

Anselmo retreated again from the room—though Harry expected not far.

She came up to him and took both of his hands in hers. "I will accept your help, Harry. Everything here has changed. I fear things have changed in ways I have not yet discovered. I am uneasy. I am grateful to you."

"I am obliged to you, Doña Isabel. For our lives."

She shrugged off the suggestion. "That is not why you should be doing this."

"From what I have learned of your father's exploits— how much he accomplished for the cause of the Union out here—I am sure President Lincoln himself would want me to help you."

"That is not why either." Isabel stood on tiptoe and kissed his cheek, Then let go his hands and stepped back. "I would have you dine with us this evening—you, and Senor Tantou."

"Gladly."

"There will be other guests."

ANSELMO joined him in the hall and escorted him to the door.

"You overheard what transpired?" Harry asked him.

"Of course. And, as you assist her, I will assist you."

"Commencing when?"

The other spread his hands in a gesture of openness. "Commencing now."

"I would like to see the room where it happened."

"Don Luis's study? That room has been locked."

"On the order of the authorities?"

"On the order of Senorita Isabel. We have not yet been able to fully clean and repair it, and the sight of what is there upsets her."

Harry held his ground at the threshhold. "Where would she be now?"

"She has not slept well, since receiving the news, and so takes her rest when she can during the day. I expect she has retired to her room."

"Give me a few minutes in Don Luis's study. Just a few."

Anselmo frowned. "I will have to stay with you."

"Of course."

THE curtains had been drawn over all the windows, with only small cracks of light at their sides penetrating the heavy gloom. As Anselmo shut the door behind them, Harry went to the windows and flung the curtains aside, blinking at the sudden glare of sunshine. Returning to the center of the large chamber, he looked to the massive desk that dominated one end.

"He was there?"

"He was found on the floor beside it."

Harry went to that spot, kneeling down. There was a dark stain that had to be blood, but it ran in almost a straight line along the wooden floorboards. There were small pockmarks in the wood.

"There was a rug here?"

"*Sí*. Senorita Isabel ordered it taken away."

Rising, Harry turned to look at the wall behind the desk. As he expected, there was a patterned disfiguration of the adobe from the shotgun blast. He went to it, drawing his finger around its outer edge, noting that it was a small pattern and that it was somewhat higher than his own head as he stood there. He looked again at the stain on the floor.

"He must have come around the desk when he was shot."

Anselmo shrugged. "He may have risen from his chair. He could have been standing where he was shot."

"Did he usually lock the door when he was in here?"

"He locked the door when he was not in here. Otherwise, it was unlocked. His children lived in this house, when they were not at the hacienda. He was fond of them and was happy to have them interrupt his work."

Harry took a walk around the room, slowly, his eyes traveling from floor to ceiling and back again.

"Some furniture has been removed?"

"A few pieces. One chair had blood on it, and worse."

"He was shot in the face?"

Anselmo nodded, sadly. Harry moved on to the other end of the room, studying the floor there carefully. There was the outline of something large and rectangular on the wood, marked by a different coloration.

"What was here?" Harry asked.

"A chest."

"I presume it wasn't spattered by blood. Where did it go?"

A quick shrug was the reply. "On the news of the Confederates' approach, Don Luis removed as many of his prized possessions from the house as he could. The chest contained things of great personal value to him."

"You're his business manager. Do you know where he took it?"

"No. I was gone—with his daughter, to Peralta."

"To wait for us?"

"I believe that's what she was to do."

"Why didn't you stay?"

"We heard reports of bad things happening here—the Texans. She was worried about her father."

"With good reason, it seems."

"Sadly, yes."

"Could one of them—the Texans—have done this?"

"I don't think so. They had left town, retreating toward Albuquerque, when Don Luis returned."

"What about Confederate sympathizers here in Santa Fe? They would have resented what Don Luis did for the Union Army."

Another shrug. Harry turned toward the big desk. "May I look in there?"

Anselmo studied the huge piece of furniture. "No, senor. I don't think Isabel would want you to."

"Why?"

"Please, senor."

"When was Don Luis's funeral?"

"Mass was said at the Mission of San Miguel a week ago."

"And he is buried there?"

The man was becoming restless and impatient, but still trying to be helpful, or to appear to be so. "No, senor. He was laid to rest at a small graveyard near La Cueva Ridge."

"Where is that?"

"Just north of Glorieta Pass. Some of the dead from the battle are buried there, too."

"Why would he be buried out there?"

"He grew up here. He loved the land by those mountains very much. It was his wish to be buried there. Believe me. He told me."

HARRY found Tantou sitting cross-legged on the boardwalk outside the hotel, leaning back against the building with his hat pulled down over his face.

"Are you awake?" Harry asked.

"Yes," said Tantou, without moving an inch.

"Have you learned anything?"

"No. Have you?"

"Yes. I think. We are invited to dinner tonight. Both of us. At the house of Don Luis." He pondered the stains on Tantou's jacket. "I don't suppose you have a more suitable suit of clothes."

"These have been very suitable."

"If you don't mind, I'll purchase you something better." Tantou raised his head. "It will be a brief inconvenience."

The Meti slowly got to his feet. "I think I will go out into the desert."

"If you please, there is something important this afternoon."

"Your friend Leahy is going to court."

"Yes. And there may be people out to mete justice in their own fashion. I would appreciate it if you could attend the session with me well armed and help me spare him such a fate."

"I do not even know this man."

"You will like him. You are like him in many ways."

"But I am not in jail, am I, Harry Raines?"

A squadron of cavalry escorted Leahy from his military confinement to the courthouse at a slow, somber walk. The troopers rode, while Leahy trudged along between them, looking very much the condemned man. Harry stood on the front veranda of the Palace of the Governors to watch the small procession pass by. Leahy seemed in both good health and spirits, but stared straight ahead, taking no note of Harry's presence.

Tantou, a brace of long-barreled pistols in his belt, stood in the plaza opposite, keeping his eyes on the crowd. Most of the people were Mexican. They seemed more curious than malevolent, though there appeared to be a few hard men in their midst.

When the military column had gone by, Harry fell in behind it, following it to the courthouse three blocks away. The sheriff had posted only one deputy at its door, a lazy-looking man who slouched against a door post.

No shot rang out. No voice was raised in anger. It occurred to Harry that word of the misidentification he had discovered from the photograph may have spread through the community. Perhaps they were merely waiting to see what the civil system of justice would make of the matter.

An elegant barouche had drawn up near the courthouse. A dark-haired woman in an abundance of clothing sat imperiously in the rear seat. A Negro maidservant sat in the front, facing the lady, while she perused the crowd. Her eyes found Harry and remained upon him. He was happy when, with the flow of people, he was able to enter the courthouse and put his back to her.

Harry had arrived too late to find a seat, but took a place against the rear wall. There commenced a considerable conversation among the spectators, and it took several raps of a bailiff's billy against the top of the judicial bench before quiet was at last imposed.

The judge was announced, and everyone stood. He was a white-haired man who wore gold-rimmed spectacles much like Harry's and bore the majesty of his office in his carriage and face.

He read aloud the charges against Leahy and asked his plea. The Irishman, who had no attorney defending him, asked to approach the bench. The request was granted.

The two leaned closed as Leahy spoke quickly—and inaudibly. Then, to Harry's amazement, Leahy reached up and shook the judge's hand. He then stepped back, standing very straight, and waited.

"This case is continued until Thursday next," the judge said. "The defendant will be released on bond of one dollar."

Leahy gave a quick shake of his head.

"No. On second thought, the fellow looks dangerous," said the judge. "No bail. Remanded to federal custody."

Chapter 18

STOPPING by the Palace of Governors on the way back to his hotel, Harry asked if he might see Captain Hosfeldt. The soldier at the door took his name and disappeared inside, returning after several minutes.

"You're to see Colonel Weimers," he said.

"But I asked to see Captain Hosfeldt."

"Captain Hosfeldt says you're to see Colonel Weimers. He's the regimental commander, and he's in charge here now and he wants to see you."

Harry was led to an anteroom with a long bench on one side and a sergeant at a desk on the other. A man in a yellow and green checked suit who might have been a whiskey drummer sat at one end of the bench, and a long-haired Indian in remnants of a cavalry uniform and a top hat sat sleeping at the other end. Decorously, Harry took a place equidistant from both and sat there feeling suddenly like a prisoner himself, wondering if he might soon be joining Leahy.

Many more minutes passed, with the Indian now commencing to snore. Of a sudden, his eyes opened, and the snoring ceased. A moment later, a door behind the sergeant opened, and a tall, thin officer with a full moustache and spectacles stepped out, still holding onto the knob.

He looked disdainfully at the man in the checked suit then shifted to Harry. "You're Harrison Raines?"

Harry stood. "Yes, sir."

The other nodded to the interior of his office, then disappeared into it.

"Shut the door," he said, as Harry entered. Harry did so. "Other fellow out there—he's a reporter. Correspondent for one of the Denver papers. Damned rascal. If I don't talk to him, he'll just make something up. They're talking of the Battle of Glorieta Pass up there as one of the epochal events of the war."

"If it has kept the West in the Union, then it was," Harry said.

"Yes. I wasn't in on much of it, fear to say. But it was a victory for certain." He seated himself. He had long arms, and easily reached across his desk for a sheaf of papers. "You asked for Hosfeldt. Any particular reason?"

"I was inquiring after the status of an associate of mine—Joseph Leahy. His trial was postponed today—for a week."

"Yes, yes. Leahy. Claims to be a federal agent."

"Actually, I made that claim, sir. For both of us. I showed Captain Hosfeldt a paper."

"Yes, indeed. A pass signed by the president. Yes. We're accepting your bonafide, Raines. And we'll be quiet about it, I promise. Do you have a rank? Are you a scout, or in the Secret Service."

"The latter, sir. And I'm a captain."

"Good, good." He rubbed his hands together vigorously, as though about to devour a tasty meal. "Now, you were in Santa Fe during the Rebel occupation?"

"No sir. I was in Peralta—down the Rio Grande aways."

"Sorry. I've been misinformed."

"We had a battle there, too. The Federal side could have captured the entire Rebel army here if they'd pressed the thing. But they didn't. The Union commander seemed to be trying to shoo the Confederates out of New Mexico."

"Well, 'out' is where they're heading. We'll chase 'em into Texas and all the way to Galveston if we have to."

"I'm not sure the Rebel troops I saw will last that long."

"Maybe not. Maybe not." He picked up the sheaf of papers. "I'm interested in something else, Raines. The local civilians. Nice thing about this back-and-forth kind of war is that it exposes things. The Rebels take control of the town, then out come the Reb sympathizers. We move back in, and there they are, caught in the open—or so we hope." He thrust the sheaf of papers at Harry. "Here's a list of them. Tell me if you know any of the names."

Harry went through it as quickly as he could: "Alfredo Anarquista, Josepha Banderillas, Mercedes Beignet, Juan Fuentes, Domingo Herrera, Carlos Martinez, Alejandro Martinez, Emiliano Vasquez, . . ."

Lafayette Baker and the provost marshal's office in Washington kept such lists, drawn up on the basis of who knew what whispers, wild rumors, barroom gossip, and outright lies motivated by a chance for profit or revenge. In Richmond, Captain Godwin and his "Plug Uglies" policed the reputed disloyal in similar fashion. People were dragged from their houses and jailed on the word of a neighbor. Many were hanged on the mere suspicion of being spies. These incidents were regular public occasions in both cities.

The Confederacy claimed it was fighting a second American revolution—to restore liberties it charged the United States had taken. The Union was waging war in the name of restoring the rule of the Constitution and the Bill of Rights—and, whether the politicians admitted it or not, to extend their protections and freedoms to another race of people.

Yet both governments were now embracing despotism. Even Mr. Lincoln, whom Harry admired above all others, had picked up the tools of oppression—jailing people without benefit of trial. Harry had assisted in the arrest of several, including an old family friend, Rose Greenhow.

"What difference does it make now if they sympathized with the South?" Harry asked. "Those Texans won't be back. From the looks of them, I'm not sure they'll all make Texas again."

"It's the reason they're for the South. The Mexicans are the big worry. They're only fourteen years in the Union. Treaty of Guadalupe Hidalgo. Year before that, when General Kearny was running things here under martial law, you know what happened up in Taos."

"Not really. I'm an Easterner." The word sounded odd. He had not used it much before.

"The Indians and Mexicans stopped fighting each other and turned on us 'Americanos.' Hundreds of them. Murdered the governor, Charles Bent. Got wiped out themselves, but it took a while. We don't want any more of that, sir. Got to calm things down."

Harry returned the list. "You have a Carlos Martinez marked down here. He and his wife are dead. I saw their bodies and identified them later from a photograph. My friend Leahy is accused of killing them."

"Dead or not. They're on the list. Recognize anyone else?"

He shook his head.

"You will be in town for some time?"

"Until Leahy is released." He didn't mention the other possibility.

"Well, right now we're just watching these people. Could use some help with the watching. That's your specialty, isn't it? The Secret Service? Watching?"

"Scouting, sir. That's my specialty. I was at Bull Run, and Ball's Bluff."

"But not Glorieta Pass."

"No. I was down in Peralta."

"Well, you're free to go, Captain. Glad to have you with us."

"Thank you, sir." Harry rose from his chair, but moved no farther. "May I see that list again?"

The colonel swiftly brought it to hand. The family name had not jumped out at him because it had been written out in full—Almaden y Cortes. Isabel Almaden y Cortes, Roberto Almaden y Cortes, Eduardo Almaden y Cortes.

"Colonel, these names," Harry said, pointing to them. "These are the children of Don Luis Almaden—the murdered man, shot down in his own house before the Union retook Santa Fe. He was a Unionist, sir. A member of the town council. A hero of the battle at Glorieta Pass."

Weimers took back the papers, frowning at the entry. Then he smiled. "Abraham Lincoln's brother-in-law is a Confederate officer, I'm told."

"Yes."

"They say you're a Virginian. Do you have relatives with the Rebels?"

"Yes I do."

"Then, there you are. We live in a strange time."

STEPPING outside, he looked both ways down the street—a habit he'd decided he'd better adopt for the rest of his stay in Santa Fe. Seeing no one from whom he had anything to fear—at least, that he knew of—he crossed the street and started across the plaza, halting suddenly just beyond the fountain. The barouche and its aristocratic passenger were parked by the entrance to his hotel. He thought of going elsewhere until she decamped, but was too tired. It was also quite possible that she had no interest in him whatsoever.

He started toward the entrance.

"You, there. Sir. If you please, a moment of your time." The accent was Southern, but Mississippi or some such. Not Virginian.

He turned and strode to the side of the carriage, treating her to a wide bow. "Ma'am?"

"Are you the Virginian they talk about?"

"I'm not certain I've made the aquaintance of 'they,' " he said. "But I am from the Old Dominion—though a long time coming to this place."

"I would like to speak with you. Would you ride with me?"

"I was heading inside."

"Just around the plaza. I won't keep you long, sir."

Her Negro maid had climbed up next to the driver. Harry took the rearward facing seat opposite. She was a strikingly handsome woman, but some years older than he. As old, perhaps, as the still comely Rose Greenhow, an old Raines family friend but also a particularly infamous Confederate spy now residing in Washington's Old Capital Prison.

"Harrison Raines, at your service, ma'am," he said, returning his hat to his head.

She extended her own hand, which he merely shook. "Mercedes Beignet. Madame Beignet."

"I'm told there is a pastry by that name—in New Orleans."

"I am from New Orleans, but I can assure you, I am not a pastry."

Harry disagreed, but kept his tongue. The coachman jolted them forward, then reined the horses back to a slow walk.

An assortment of thoughts seemed to be running very rapidly through her mind. He sensed that one she considered and then discarded had to do with amour, a notion that doubtless came to her mind with every gentleman she encountered. But there were more serious matters. In a moment, the sparkle in her eyes was lost in the gloom of worry.

"I know three things about you," she said. "One is that you have just been with the Yankee commander. Another is that you are acquainted with the Yankee who's being held as the murderer of Don Carlos Martinez and are trying to have him freed. The last is that you were taken from here one recent night by the Mexican underground, and yet returned alive."

"What Mexican underground?" he asked, though he knew perfectly well to whom she was referring.

"A secret society. Many of them the very best society—Mexican society. The Dons. The landholders. They had common cause with the Confederacy for a time, but now I am not sure. A friend of mine was one of them. You know his daughter, I see."

"His daughter?" They were rounding the far end of the plaza. Young girls, some of them accompanied by duennas, were strolling along the walk.

"You called on her today. Isabel Almaden. Her father was a dear friend of mine. Very dear. But he betrayed me. He betrayed us all. If the Confederate cause had prevailed at Glorieta, he would have been shot."

"He was shot, madame."

"Yes he was, the poor man, but not by the Confederate army."

"Then by whom?"

A passing coach, leather window closings down, caught her attention. "I have no idea," she said, turning back.

"But you seem to know everything, Madame Beignet."

She smiled, but not sweetly. "Among the many things I do not know, is something about you, Virginian."

They were coming by the Palace of the Governors now. Colonel Weimers was standing on the gallery, smoking a cigar. He grinned as the carriage passed by.

"What is that, madame?"

"To which side belongs your loyalty? Virginia's, or that officer's."

"It is not always necessary to have a side."

"In a war it is."

"Let me answer you this way. I will share some information with you. Your name is on a list—a list the Federals have of Confederate sympathizers."

She laughed, so loudly a man turned toward them in the street. "Mr. Raines—if 'Mr.' it is—they don't need my name on a list. I flew the Stars and Bars from my house. I took it down only because they made me—not because I was afraid of being found out."

"What would they do to you?" He recalled that when General Benjamin Butler was the Union officer commanding in Baltimore, he had threatened cannon fire on the homes of the local ladies of society if they did not remove their Confederate emblems.

"To me? Nothing. I am a respectable lady of the town. I've committed no crime. They have treated me with respect so far. I'd be far more worried about the Mexicans."

"What Mexicans?"

"The Mexicans on the list. And Mexicans not on the list. There are some dangerous games afoot. I fear my friend Don Luis Almaden may have been a loser in one."

"Isn't there anything you can tell me of his death?"

"Only that I cried all day long at the news. I am surprised that his children have shown so little emotion."

"His children? Have you seen his sons?"

"No. They are away. They did not come back for his funeral mass. None of them did."

"Isabel was with me. South, in Peralta. She had no word of her father's fate until we came to Santa Fe, and that was after his funeral. Where were his sons?"

"It is said they were serving with the New Mexican militia, but no one believes that."

"Why wasn't he buried at the church here? Why so far out in the country?"

"It was his wish." She looked as though another day of crying might soon be upon her.

They were nearing the hotel. "I'm sorry you have been distressed, madame. You need not worry about me. I'll cause you no problem. If I can be a help to you, I will. If there is something you can tell me about Don Carlos Martinez or Don Luis Almaden, I would appreciate that greatly. I am staying at this hotel."

"On the second floor." She pointed to his window. "There." She eased back into a corner of the seat. "Good day to you then, 'Mr.' Raines."

Chapter 19

HARRY loaned Tantou his other new suit for the evening and was surprised to find the fit a little loose. The Meti was one of those men who looked much larger than he was—something he had in common with General Robert E. Lee. For his part, Tantou indicated he would be unhappy in this clothing no matter if the fit were exactly perfect. The wearing of it was merely something to endure, like the cold desert wind.

Anselmo, finely dressed himself, greeted them at the door and ushered them into a candlelit parlor. There, Isabel, in a black lace dress, in keeping with her mourning but bare-shouldered, welcomed them, a sad expression on her face, and introduced them to the guests who had arrived before them.

One was Lieutenant Colonel Manuel Chavez, written of in both the Spanish and English language newspapers as a hero of Glorieta, wearing a splendid militia officer's uniform of dark blue with red sash and sword. There were two couples, a Senor and Senora Emiliano Vasquez and a Senor and Senora Simon de Montebello, and a very stern looking elderly woman, whom Isabel introduced as her grandmother.

Vasquez, a plain, almost peasant-like man, whom Isabel described as a close friend of her father's, appeared uneasy, and kept glancing about the room, as though for Don Luis's spectre. His wife, Inez, small and plump, was chatty and given to a high-pitched laugh. Montebello and his wife, Alicia, a sleekly older and more finished version of Isabel, were far more cosmopolitan. He spoke English flawlessly; she, when she heard Tantou's accent, conversed with him in excellent French. Harry could only wonder what the two found to talk about.

The adobe fireplace had no mantel—its only decoration a silver crucifix. Harry stepped away from the others, toward Tantou, using the movement to look about the room. He saw what he sought on a high top table in the corner, lit by a candle, the whole of it resembling very much a shrine.

As unobtrusively as possible, he made his way to the framed glass photographic plate, leaning close to it, for he was not wearing his spectacles and it was small. Finally, having no choice, he picked it up and held it near the candle.

He heard a rustle of silk.

"That is my father," Isabel said. She took the picture from him, holding it with great care.

"He looks young. I thought it was your brother."

"Oh no. He was not young. But he was very handsome. That keeps away the years."

"And he was a good friend of Don Carlos Martinez?"

"Oh yes. Our families are very close."

"Would Don Carlos have let him borrow his best horse?"

"The palomino? *Sí. Por supuesto.* They were like brothers. Why do you ask? Has this something to do with the Irishman who is in jail?"

"No, not precisely."

"I love my father, Harry."

"I know. That's why I'm trying to help you find his killer."

"This is not the time for that." She set the photograph back in its place. "Let us go in to dinner."

GRACE was said, at Isabel's request, by Anselmo, who had abandoned any vestige of the servant and taken a seat at the table at Isabel's right, facing Harry, who sat on her left. It was an eloquent address to God, rendered in both Spanish and English, offering thanks for their survival of the war that had come and gone so swiftly, praying for the souls of the dead, praying for the lives of those who still lived.

Isabel gave him a soft smile of approval, then stood, wine glass in hand. "I have invited you all here because you are family or friends of my father, who was as brave and noble a man as we ever will meet. Not all of us were able to attend the mass said for him, or accompany him to his grave. But we can remember him on this pleasant evening—an occasion of which I've no doubt he'd approve, a celebration of our deliverance from the armies of slavery." She nodded to Colonel Chavez. "We must all be thankful to so many who risked their lives in battle, so that we might enjoy the freedom this night to freely gather here."

She nodded now to Harry and to Tantou. "My thanks to Mr. Harrison Raines, and Monsieur Tantou. Without them, I should not be here at all."

To Harry's view, it had been quite the other way around. As for Isabel's father, he certainly had reason to admire the man, but, having never met him, could not find reason for his inclusion in this circle of beloved. He sat there, puzzled, wondering when this odd toast would be concluded—and how a woman listed as a suspected Confederate could speak so disdainfully of the Southern cause.

"So, I will raise my glass to my father, and to so many others as committed to the cause of justice as he was." She waited, as the dinner guests got to their feet. Tantou, seated next to Harry, sat staring at his plate until Harry gave him a discreet kick in the foot. With some slowness, he stood.

They all drank. The wine was excellent.

As Leahy had found jails and prisoner of war camps fertile ground for information gathering, Harry had learned the usefulness of dinner parties. He had learned this lesson after the fact, having attended Rose Greenhow's Washington soirees for nearly three years before her arrest, and its consequent revelations made him realize her purpose—and understand her methods.

She used these occasions in two ways, plucking often vital information from streams of casual conversation, and also as opportunities to charm high-ranking military officers and important politicians and initiate relationships with them. Former President James Buchanan, though hardly a likely target for her sexual wiles, had been addicted to her charm and was a constant visitor. So had been Secretary of State Seward.

Harry did not count charm or sexual wiles among his Secret Service assets, but dinner conversation was a part of Tidewater plantation life he'd grown up in. Judging Colonel Chavez likely to be the most knowledgeable, he waited until the officer's attention was turned his way and then commented on how pleased President Lincoln would be to learn how steadfastly loyal the New Mexico population had been to the Union.

"For the most part, that is true," he said. "The people here want nothing to do with the despotism the Confederates represent. We settled that question in the last war, when we got rid of Santa Ana and became Americans."

"It wasn't everyone who wanted to get rid of Santa Ana," said Vasquez. "We could have used him now, in fighting these Texans."

"*No me jodas!*" said Chavez. "We swept the Texans before us with ease. Major Chivington is the equal of General Winfield Scott or Sam Houston. Maybe better. Santa Ana would not have lasted a day against him."

"*Exactamente!*" said Vasquez. "Your Union Army is the same as the one sent by President Polk."

The suave Don Simon de Montebello attempted to avert further discord. "It is true that there is an irony here. In 1846, many of the families of Santa Fe opposed the United States annexation—and fought the invading army. It was made up largely of Southerners. Now the United States joins us in fighting these same Southern people."

Vasquez glowered. An argument ensued that was waged entirely in rapid Spanish—the elderly grandmother following it with hard black eyes, which spoke many words worth of malice.

"This goes on all the time," said Isabel to Harry. "*Siem-*

pre." She touched his arm. The candles on the table cast a golden glow on the curve of her breasts above the décolletage of her dress. "Thank you for coming tonight. It is nice to have your company in a civilized circumstance. Unlike on the trail."

"I did not mind the trail."

"I am glad that you are staying in Santa Fe for a while."

"A few days."

"But I worry about you. Matters are not settled here. Perhaps you should think about leaving sooner. I would hate to see you go, but there are dangers. If the Union Army should go back to Colorado . . ."

Harry looked to Tantou, who was using both knife and fork—the latter strictly to hold the meat as he cut it. "I have a formidable ally in this gentleman—as you may recall."

"I do recall."

"And you?" he said. "You are all alone here. I worry about you as well."

"I am not alone." She turned to her right. "I have Anselmo. And, somewhere—my brothers."

The family retainer looked pleased. "The men of the hacienda who were with the militia, they are coming home now," he said. "Is that not so, Colonel?"

Chavez turned from the other discussion. *"Sí. Pronto."*

Anselmo smiled. "So it will be safe."

Harry sought Isabel's complete attention, leaning close. "Lincoln," he whispered.

She gazed at him pleasantly, looking utterly puzzled.

"You are to say, 'Juárez.' "

"Oh yes. Gladly. Juárez."

"Why are those two names linked?"

"I believe the two gentlemen think very highly of one another. If it were not for the war here, I am certain President Lincoln would be helping President Juárez now."

"There is a civil war in Mexico." There had been articles in the Washington papers—before Sumter.

"That is mostly over—mostly won. The problem now is France. Juárez suspended payments on foreign debts, and England, Spain, and France last fall landed troops at Vera Cruz to lay claim to their money, taking it from custom house receipts. But France wants more—that horrid *empereur* of theirs. He has sent an entire army, and we fear it is bent on conquest."

"You seem very well versed in this matter, senorita."

"No more than you about this nation."

"This is not your nation?"

The remark was a trespass. A coolness came over them as though from a door opened in the dead of winter. He moved to close it.

"Tell me about Juárez. Is he as wise a man as our Lincoln?"

"I don't know that your Lincoln is so wise. How could this war go on so long if he were? But I know that Mr. Lincoln is a kind man, and I think that he and Juárez are equally kind. Both came from the poorest backgrounds. Juárez is from Zapotec Indians—peasants. Lincoln grew up in a rude wooden hut, no?"

"A log cabin."

"Well, there you are. Not like Santa Ana. Not like the French *empereur*."

"Your father admired Juárez?"

"Oh yes. He . . ." She looked to Chavez, who had been following their conversation closely.

Harry spoke up quickly. "A question, Colonel. Someone today asked by about the Taos Revolt. I know nothing about it."

Now all conversation at the table ceased.

"I know something about it," Chavez said.

"He knows everything about it," said Vasquez. "He was there."

"You took part in the revolt?" Harry asked.

Chavez smiled pleasantly. "No."

"He fought for General Kearny against the revolt," Vasquez said. "At Santa Cruz de la Canada and Embudo. Hundreds were killed."

"That is perhaps an exaggeration," said Montebello.

"*Para nada!*" said Vasquez. "It was a slaughter."

"What was the revolt about?" Harry asked quickly.

Montebello spread his hands. "Many reasons. You Americanos came into New Mexico peacefully, but peace did not long obtain. Nothing was done to protect the local population against the Navajos, who were on a rampage."

"Navajos took part in the revolt," Chavez said.

"That was later," said Vasquez. "After the gringos were on the run." He took note of Harry. "*Lo siento.* I mean, the bad gringos."

"Kearny's men were well behaved," said Montebello. "But some of the Texas volunteers . . ."

"The Taos Rebels murdered the governor—many public officials," Chavez said to Harry. "It was the first thing they did. January 19, 1847, was the date. In Taos, that was where it began."

"It spread all over *Neuvo Mexico,*" said Vasquez, "but it didn't last a month."

"It began in Taos and ended there," Montebello said. "At the church of San Jeronimo."

"What did you say?" Harry asked.

"The church of San Jeronimo. At Taos."

"The last stand," added Vasquez. "Many died. Many were taken prisoner. Nearly two dozen were hanged after that."

"*Mi eposo!*"

These two words brought all conversation to a halt. They came from the lips of the hard-eyed old woman, who had directed the words at the colonel. No one spoke until she relented, returning to her meal.

"My grandfather was condemned," said Isabel. "But he was not hanged. He was killed in his cell. No one knows who did it."

"The *Americanos* did it," Vasquez said.

"All that was regrettable," said Chavez. "All of it. But what would the revolt have accomplished? Many Mexicans fought against Santa Ana. He was doomed to lose. He could not have held Mexico. His defeat was inevitable. Now, we have democracy. And no slavery."

"This church of San Jeronimo, it's not where your father is buried?" Harry asked Isabel.

"No, Harry."

"His resting place is at La Cueva," said Anselmo. "By Glorieta. It is fitting."

"*Por supuesto,*" said Chavez, raising his glass. "To Don Luis. He is your true liberator."

As everyone drank, there was a sudden commotion in the hall. An excited servant ran by the doorway. A moment later, a young man in hat, riding cloak, and dusty boots appeared there, his dark eyes glittering as he took note of every face in the room.

"Roberto!" cried Isabel. She pushed back her chair and stood up, her face a picture of disbelief.

With her brother's arrival, dinner concluded. He did not linger long in the doorway, but dashed off to the other end of the hall. A door slammed. Isabel excused herself and went off in pursuit.

The housemaid who had served the several courses consumed thus far reappeared with a tray bearing what looked to be dessert. Shaking his head, Anselmo said something quickly in Spanish, and she left.

Vasquez stood. "Where has Roberto been?"

"We don't know," Amselmo said. "Senorita Isabel was afraid he was dead." He looked to the grandmother. "Doña Magarita?"

The old woman replied in Spanish, rising from her chair and leaving the room—heading not toward the front door but in the direction Isabel had gone.

The other guests all rose, somewhat disconcertedly.

Anselmo sought to bridge the breach of etiquette, a violation of hospitality that Harry gathered would not have been tolerated by Don Luis. "If the ladies would care to refresh themselves." A gesture to the hall. "For the gentlemen, I will serve Fundador and cigars—in the parlor." Doubtless Don Luis would have chosen his study.

Vasquez waved his hand dismissively, taking his wife's arm with the other. *"Buenos noches."*

An amused look came over Alicia Montebello's face. She slipped her hand inside her husband's elbow, turning him. Harry thought they were departing the house as well, but the couple went into the parlor instead. Chavez and Harry followed, with Tantou coming along quietly behind.

Anselmo poured brandy all around, then produced a large wooden box of cigars. All but Tantou and Senora Montebello accepted. Alicia Montebello produced a small silver case of her own, taking from it a short slender cigar for herself, which her husband lighted.

She came over to Harry, seeming delighted with all that had transpired. "All this is very crazy, no?"

"It's in keeping with my other experiences here in the West."

"Tumultuous times. Two wars in a single generation." She sipped the strong brandy without falter. "I am afraid that few of us here understand this one."

"It is more understandable back East."

"Fewer Negroes here."

"You will see more, if they are ever allowed to become soldiers in the Union Army."

"I have spoken only ever to two. Both servants of Madame Beignet. I believe you are acquainted."

"Only very recently."

"The plaza is a very public place."

"So I have come to understand."

"She was a prostitute, you know."

"Madame Beignet?"

"In New Orleans. She rose quickly in that profession and opened her own establishment. Made quite a lot of money. The sheriff told me." She languorously exhaled a veil-like cloud of cigar smoke.

"How did she find her way here?"

"She married well, but briefly. Her husband died suddenly. Her move from New Orleans to here had something to do with that. This I heard from Judge Ambrose."

Before Harry could pursue these revelations, Chavez motioned to him to join a conversation the colonel was having with Montebello. Senora Montebello went to Tantou, who was standing alone in the corner, holding his brandy glass awkwardly with both hands.

"Senor Montebello wants to know who you think will win the war," Chavez said.

Anselmo joined them.

"If the Union fights as you did at Glorieta, it will win," Harry said.

"But it has not gone well in the East," Montebello said.

"They have a poor general." Harry reminded himself he was speaking of Mr. Pinkerton's immediate superior, General George B. McClellan.

"The South has a good one?"

"A few."

"And here?"

Harry realized they were asking more of him than his opinion of general officers.

"I've not encountered any."

Anselmo, pointedly, had not refreshed glasses and had left no bottle in view. Montebello set down his empty glass and touched his wife's arm. She finished her drink, and they were soon gliding toward the foyer. Chavez, a little reluctantly, followed, as did Harry and Tantou, the latter still holding his glass.

The Montebellos' coach was brought first, then Chavez's saddle horse. Before mounting, reins in hand, he stepped close to Harry.

"I am aware that you are one of us, Captain Raines— that you work with the Union Army," he said. "I will of course keep your secret. If you are indeed going to be with us for a while longer, we may call upon you. There are many matters still not finished here."

"I will be of small use to you without the assistance of my colleague."

"This Indian? Monsieur Tantou?"

"Joseph Leahy."

"I don't think you need worry." He smiled and climbed aboard his horse. *"Adiós."*

Harry and Tantou had walked to the Almaden house. Harry turned to look for someone to say goodnight to and saw Isabel standing on the doorstep.

"Buenas noches," he said. *"Muchas gracias.* You see. I am learning."

"No, Harry. I'd like you to stay."

"But your brother has just come home."

"He has gone away again. Please. You must stay the night."

"Isabel. My hotel is but a few blocks away."

"You cannot go there. Please. It is not safe." She looked up and down the street. "Those people who took you away."

"You know about that?"

"Roberto told me. They want you again, Harry, and this time they may be more serious. It is about the gold your man Leahy stole."

"Not 'stole.' Recovered. It's hidden."

"Then they will be very serious indeed. Please, come in. Stay until morning."

Harry took a deep breath, happy and apprehensive at the same time. "What about Tantou?"

"Him, too. *Desde luego.*"

"A moment." He went to Tantou, who was still holding his glass. "The lady invites us to spend the night. She says my Mexican hosts of the other night are seeking my company again."

"Then you are a good man to stay away from, Harry Raines."

"Jack. She said us both."

The Meti drank all of his brandy in a few swallows, showing no sign of its addition to his chemistry. He handed the empty glass to Harry. "I am becoming weary of hotels and houses. I think I will go for a ride."

"Tonight? Where?"

"Around. Look for things."

Isabel had gone back inside, but was lingering just inside the door.

"There is something I'd like you to look for," Harry said. "The dead couple were in a farm wagon. I want you to look for a farm wagon."

"But we know where that wagon was. You want me to ride back down the Rio Grande to see if it is still there?"

"No. I want you to ride out to the Almaden hacienda and see if there is one there."

Tantou looked off into the darkness, as if he could see all the way to the hacienda. "If there is not one, it means little. The Rebels could have taken it like they have taken so much."

"But if there is one, then I needn't think some of the things I'm thinking now."

SHE stood alone in the hall. Harry shut the door behind him, waiting for her to speak, but she did not. Taking a step toward him, she ran both her hands up his arms to his shoulders and then pulled him to her. It was a far different kind of kiss than she had given him before.

She remained in his arms afterward, her head against his shoulder. He felt a little dizzy—and very confused.

"Your brother is gone?"

"Yes. And my grandmother has gone to bed. There is only Anselmo—and Lucia, the maid."

"I shall ruin your reputation."

"There are worse things to fear. I was not completely honest with you. I am afraid for you, but I am also afraid for myself."

"Your brother?"

"He is very upset. About my father. About everything. But there is more."

Harry stroked her hair. He felt as though he could stand there doing that all night. "The secret society," he said, finally.

She pulled back. "What do you know of that?"

"Only what Madame Beignet told me. And what I saw with my own eyes—much as they'd let me."

A clock chimed. Harry wondered why it hadn't been taken by the fleeing Rebels.

"Did you bring a gun?"

Harry pulled a Navy Colt from the pocket of his coat. "One."

"Anselmo has weapons." She paused. "I'm hoping that won't be necessary."

SHE led him to a large bedroom off the upstairs hall, kissed him goodnight, and went off down the hall without another word. He waited a few moments, but she did not return.

He put his Navy Colt on the nightstand, then undressed and got into bed. It was the most comfortable he had been in since leaving Virginia weeks before, but he found he could not sleep. His window overlooked the street and had a view of Santa Fe rooftops extending to the plaza. He could see torchlight over there, brighter than that from the oil lamps.

He lay back, finally slipping into the first of sleep, but was almost immediately disturbed by a loud noise. He thought it might have something to do with the torchlights, but realized it had been inside the house.

He heard a man's voice and two more loud noises. Then it was quiet again. He decided it was Roberto, who had probably been drinking when he had barged in at dinner and had been drinking more.

He managed to sleep again, but when he was awakened once more, it was as though to a dream. The bedcovers stirred, the bed sagged slightly, there was a wonderful sweet scent and then the softness of cotton and the warmth of bare human flesh. Her hair came over his face as she leaned to kiss him.

He put his arm around her. "I am amazed. I am overjoyed. But I delude myself. You are here because you are frightened."

She kissed him again and snuggled close. "No, that is not why I am here. I am here because this is the first time I have had such a chance to be with you. To be with you like this."

"On the trail . . ."

"Not there. I am a lady, Harrison Raines."

"I have noticed."

"And I did not know you so well."

"I still do not know you well."

"Well enough, *me amante.*"

Her cotton nightgown came up over her head.

Chapter 20

SHE left his bed before sunrise, as he supposed was only appropriate for a lady of her standing in a society that prized church virtue above all else. Harry put his hand where she had lain, happy to find a lingering warmth. Less happily, he reminded himself of what he had to do that day.

He sat up, groggier than he expected to be. He'd had more of drink and much less of sleep than he'd thought. Shaking his head vigorously, he went to the basin on the nightstand and began splashing water on himself. He had no clean shirt, but had only put this one on the evening before. In this wild country, a week in the same garment was nothing to remark upon.

Fully dressed, his Navy Colt back in place and boots in hand, Harry stepped into the hall, listening and looking but finding only silence and closed doors. He had no idea which was Isabel's and was in no mind to explore, lest he come upon the temperamental Roberto instead.

In stocking feet, he descended to the main hall, where

he seated himself on a caned chair and pulled on his boots. He was about to leave by the front door when it occurred to him he needed to leave her a note.

The door to Don Luis's study was unlocked, and the room seemed not to have been disturbed since his last visit. Harry went to the desk, opening drawers until he found writing paper and pen and ink.

He wrote quickly:

Isabel,
Sadly, I must leave you, though you have made me the happiest of men. I mean to keep my word about helping you find your father's killer, and I am going to start with the place where he is buried—if I can find it. I think I understand what has happened. I hope to return soon and will ask Colonel Weimers for protection for you in the meantime.

Love,
Harry

He folded the letter and was rummaging for sealing wax when he saw the door move. Somewhat clumsily, Harry took his pistol to hand, but not before Anselmo had entered holding a double-barreled shotgun pointed Harry's way. The two observed each other almost thoughtfully. Then Harry lowered his pistol, setting it on the desk and resuming his search. Ignoring Anselmo as the other came forward, he at last found what he sought. Holding it over the folded letter, he struck a match and put it to the stick of wax, letting it drip.

"This is for Senorita Isabel," he said.

"I did not think it was for me."

"I'm leaving. I suppose you will be glad of that."

"She will not. Though I suppose you are coming back."

"Perhaps."

"You were going through Don Luis's desk."

"Looking only for this." Harry waved the stick of wax and returned it to its drawer. What he said was the truth, but he'd noticed something that interested him: a glass plate photograph of Don Luis's three children, which had been smashed and badly cracked.

Harry stood up, put his pistol back in his belt, and handed the letter to Anselmo.

"If you could see that this gets to Senorita Isabel—and not her brother Roberto."

"He has gone, senor. For the moment."

"Me, too, then. Good-bye, Anselmo. You are a good host and an interesting man. This family is lucky to have you."

"I have only seen to Isabel's wishes."

Harry moved past him. "*Adiós,* Anselmo."

"*Adiós.*"

TANTOU had slept on the floor of Harry's hotel room, but with the blanket from the bed wrapped around him. He reacted slowly and unhappily to Harry's prodding him with his boot.

"Someday someone may shoot you because you do that, Harry Raines."

"I only do that to friends."

"Someday you may no longer have friends."

The Meti sat up, rubbing his eyes. Harry perched on the bed. "Where are the horses?"

"In the stable. Mine is saddled. Yours is not."

"What did you learn last night?"

"I learned that you passed the night in a better way than me."

"A man of infinite wit." His shoulder still hurt from the hatchet. He massaged the muscle, his thoughts drifting to the previous night before he yanked them back to business again. "I was asking about the Almadens' farm wagon."

"It is there, on the hacienda."

"It's not a new one?"

"No. Much weathered."

"Hmmm."

"More interesting is what I discovered in the Almadens' coach house."

"And what did you discover?"

"That there is no coach in the coach house. I am told it is one of the most expensive in Santa Fe. But it is gone."

"Isabel did not mention it."

"That is interesting also." Tantou stood, letting the blanket fall to the floor. He had changed back into his trail clothes.

Harry gestured to a table by the door, where he had left a napkin-covered basket. "There's some fruit and some cornbread. Breakfast. Why don't you do your washing up and then eat it. I'm going to stop by the Palace of the Governors for a brief while."

"Then what?"

"Then I thought we'd go for a ride."

"We go to Denver?"

"Not quite so far. Just Glorieta Pass."

"What for?"

"I want to visit a graveyard."

"There are graveyards in Denver."

"Not like this one."

*   *   *

COLONEL Weimers was at his desk, reading what looked to be dispatches. He looked up and smiled as Captain Hosfeldt ushered Harry in.

"We have a whole Federal army coming this way from California," he said. "Word is that when they get here, we get to go back to Colorado. I was afraid they were going to make us go on down to Texas."

"It has its attractions."

"If so, it also has what's left of the Rebs who were here—a people with whom I require no further congress. Scorpions, too. Armadillos. Giant rabbits. And the world's largest collection of dust. No sir, give me Colorado. The land is green. Aspen forests. Clean streams. The only trouble comes from a few Indians and drunken miners."

"I need to speak with my friend Joseph Leahy again."

"And so you shall, sir. I shall be pleased if you do. He is free to go whenever he wishes, but he persists in his incarceration voluntarily. I have no doubt he is the federal agent—uh, scout—you say him to be, but I am also of the opinion he has gone mad from sunstroke or the like. I tried to move him from the Rebel prisoners, but he would not budge."

"How is it he is to go free?"

"Cavalry patrol found the body of the man he supposedly killed. Under a pile of rocks. There were papers on him identifying him as a representative of the Mexican government."

"Papers? Where?"

"Inside the sweat band of his hat. Someone put it under the rocks with him."

Harry had done that, placing the hat solemnly on the man's chest—stupidly neglecting to examine it.

"Did they learn his name?"

"Pablo Sanchez."

"Did your cavalry patrol learn what he was doing with Don Carlos Martinez's horse?"

"Dispatch didn't say. Fort Craig just wants to know if the fellow had been up here. Has to be some sort of official explanation sent to Mexico, though there's some question as to which Mexican government he represented. Did you know him?"

"Our acquaintance was brief. He spoke only two words to me. 'San Jeronimo.' It is the name of a church in Taos. There was a big fight there—the last stand of the Taos Revolt."

"That right?"

"Was anything else found on his person?"

"Nope. No wallet. No money. Nothing. Guess he had his pockets turned out by someone before you got to him."

The man's possessions were still in Harry's saddlebag.

"I guess I'd better talk to Mr. Leahy now," Harry said.

"AREN'T you tired of living in prisons?" Harry asked, as he and Leahy stepped out into the adjoining corral. "You have become as fixated upon these poor wretches as sources of information as Mr. Pinkerton is upon escaped slaves."

"With good reason. I have found out more important facts, Harry. There are not but two thousand Confederates now between New Mexico and the Texas capital. All the rest have been sent east to the Louisiana border."

Leahy dropped to the ground and commenced a round

of calisthenics, calling out a count as he repeatedly raised himself by arms and shoulders and then dropped to the earth again. Harry had no choice but to stand there awkwardly, while the Irishman completed fifty of these efforts.

"I'm going into the Glorieta Pass today," Harry said.

"Why?"

"I want to find a grave. I would like you to come with me."

Leahy nimbly got to his feet. "What for?"

"I don't know what else I'll find."

"This has to do with the Mexican girl."

"It has to do with the murder of her father."

"Very well," Leahy said. "But I shall have to make arrangements with the judge."

"You need not. There are no charges against you. It's been established that the man we found was not Don Carlos Martinez. He was a Pablo Sanchez—from Mexico."

"Are we not to be charged with his death, then? Some violation of federal statute."

"I most fervently hope not, Joseph. And, if that absurd development is in prospect then all the more reason we should leave from this place."

Leahy began another round of exercises, rising and falling from a squatting position. "That's where they had their great battle," Leahy said. "Glorieta. Triumph for the Union."

"Yes."

They started back toward the warehouse that had been transformed into a prison.

"Harry. I have no horse now."

"We can easily attend to that."

"With that gold we took off this Pablo Sanchez?"

They were passing through the doorway. "Joseph, this is no place for such talk."

"You still have that one-eyed nag?"

"Nag he's not, but I do."

"I keep forgetting you really are a horse trader. No wonder Mr. Pinkerton puts such store by your ability to lie and deceive."

Chapter 21

WITH the Confederate departure, good horseflesh was again available in Santa Fe, and Harry was able to procure Leahy a serviceable mount. With Tantou leading, they reached the western end of the pass by mid-afternoon. The ride from town had been without incident. Looking back from vantage points along the road, they saw no one in pursuit.

Tantou had trotted up ahead and now stopped his horse at the top of the next rise.

"You trust that man?" Leahy asked moving up beside Harry.

He'd introduced them formally, with both men responding a little warily. Tantou had seemed impressed by Leahy's obvious physical strength. Leahy had looked upon the Indian almost as though he were an apparition.

"I told you that I do," Harry said.

"He has the eye of a sharper," said the Irishman.

"He has a sharp eye. He is an excellent tracker."

"Well, what is he doing now?"

The Indian sat his horse facing right, not toward the canyon and Glorieta Pass but toward the broad mesa to the south of it.

Harry and Leahy hurried the horses up. "What is wrong?" Harry asked. "Are we lost?"

"No. I smell something bad."

Harry sniffed. "Cooking?"

"No, Harry Raines. Someone is burning dead horses."

Tantou spurred his own. The others followed. Moving along the rise as it angled toward the mesa, they soon were able to see smoke rising from above a patch of cottonwood trees. There were some ranch buildings and a few chimneys, but the smoke was coming from a clearing adjacent. Moving along farther until they could look down upon the scene, they noted a sizable contingent of blue-coated soldiers laboring with mules in a clearing beside a huge bonfire. The men wore kerchiefs around their faces, looking more like bandits than soldiers.

Piles of dead horses were all about, and around them, already consumed by fire, were the remnants of numerous wagons and other vehicles. Happily, there was no sign of human remains.

"A strange looking battle scene," said Leahy. "Is this where the Rebels were defeated?"

"It's why they were defeated," Harry said.

"That was their supply train," said Tantou. "Union Army came and burned it. Slaughtered the animals. Made a big mess."

"The Rebels had no choice but to retreat, then. Don Luis Almaden and Colonel Chavez brought the Union troops over that mesa to do this work."

"Are we near Almaden's grave?" Leahy asked.

"No," said Harry. He produced his map.

"Deeper into the canyon," Tantou said. He flicked his reins.

THE trail led back through some trees and then down the other side of the long ridge, switching back and forth into a deepening defile that grew narrower and steeper the farther they advanced into it. Tantou now took to watching the slopes to either side of them, his hand near his revolver.

"This is the Santa Fe Trail," Harry said. "Leads to Colorado."

"I know," Leahy said. "You would think you'd meet up with traffic—army patrols, if nothing else."

"Perhaps we will."

Harry took note of some circling black birds off to the east and south. Leahy saw them, too.

"I heard some bad news while I was with those Rebel prisoners," the Irishman said.

"What other kind of news is there in a military prison?"

"This came from a Union officer. It's old news, now, but no less a weep."

Harry frowned. When Leahy did not continue, he said, "What is it, Joseph?"

"The boy, Harry. Lincoln's boy?"

"Tad? What's happened to him?"

"It's the other—the quiet one. Willie. He died—of some fever."

Harry remembered a time waiting in the anteroom of Lincoln's second floor White House office—the president turning up from a walk with the young Tad on his shoulders and the solemn-looking Willie holding his hand. The boy wrote poetry. Harry recalled one he wrote in honor of a young fallen officer whom Lincoln had befriended. "A hard death to bear," he said.

"The hardest. It's a wonder he goes on. They were already down one son."

A sudden clatter of hooves around a bend ahead snapped their attention to the front. There were many horses, moving fast, emerging suddenly on the trail as a body of blue-coated horsemen. Harry and his companions drew aside as they thundered past—a courier, with an escort. One soldier returned Harry's wave but the rest paid them no mind.

"They seem full of confidence," Leahy said. "Makes one wish they'd stick around."

Tantou took one of his revolvers in hand and nudged his horse into motion.

As they passed farther into the steep-sided canyon, they began to encounter the litter of war—pieces of clothing, discarded equipment, even weapons, lying where they'd been tossed or dropped. Noticing a Confederate cartridge box and belt, Harry considered retrieving it as a souvenir, but rejected the idea as ghoulish. There'd be enough of those items lying upon the blood-soaked fields near Washington. He needn't import more from this place.

A wide break appeared in the canyon wall to the left— an arroyo leading up toward the forward slope of the Sangre de Cristo range, a narrow track paralleling the dry, raw-cut gorge that would doubtless be filled with rushing water with the next thunderstorm.

There was no hint of that. Harry consulted his map, squinting. "This has to be it."

"I can't believe there's habitation here for any man— living or dead," Leahy said.

Tantou was already starting up the arroyo.

* * *

THEY found the church—little more than a rude adobe chapel—less than a mile from the main canyon. The track was steep. The chapel sat on a ledge-like height, with a view to the southwest that included much of the ground they had just covered. It was a perfect hideout for desperados.

Dismounting, they poked around the front of the church, then went around to the back, where they found a small graveyard, overgrown with scrubby weeds.

Almaden's grave revealed itself as a clear patch with freshly turned dirt. A stone grave marker had been emplaced, bearing Don Luis's name and dates with stark, deep-cut carving. It had been poorly set, however, and was tilting somewhat backwards. Tantou went to the rear and pushed it forward again.

"You needn't have bothered," Harry said. "I'm afraid we're going to have to dislodge it again."

"Why is that, laddy buck?" Leahy asked.

"Because I want to open up the grave. We didn't come here to lay flowers."

"We didn't bring flowers," observed Leahy.

"You spend the night with her and now you dig up her father?" Tantou said. "*Vous êtes fou*, Harry Raines."

"We didn't bring a shovel," the Irishman said.

"There may be one in the church," Harry said. He began walking to the front of the building again.

They had to break in, though this was easily accomplished. There was a dusty collection box on the wall, and Harry put a coin in it as compensation.

Tantou moved on to the rear of the chamber, finding a closet of sorts. Within it were a broom and a shovel with a shortened, broken handle. Harry sighed. The day was becoming hot. It would not be an easy labor.

With Harry wielding the shovel first, they took turns at the grave. It was slow going digging such hard, rocky soil.

Leahy, whose turn was next, finished the job, waving Tantou off. "I need the exercise," he said. "Too long in that warehouse."

Brushing the last of the dirt off the top of the coffin with the broom that Tantou had thoughtfully fetched from the chapel, Leahy stepped back off the grave.

"You say he was a wealthy man?" he asked.

"One of the richest in Santa Fe," Harry said.

"Mighty cheap coffin for such a toff."

"Let's open it."

"That's sacrilege," said Tantou.

"Maybe not."

There was nothing at all resembling a crowbar to be had, and Tantou refused to allow the use of the rifle in his saddle scabbard as a pry. Finally, Leahy went and found a large rock, which he threw down with great violence against the latch of the coffin.

He smiled when this succeeded, then hopped down to lift the lid. "You ready for this, boyo?"

Harry recalled the couple in the buckboard—a memory that was quickly overwhelmed by others of pig-eaten remains on the field at Manassas and piles of contorted bodies at the base of Ball's Bluff, where the Union soldiers had been cut down trying to find a way across the deep, swift Potomac. "I suppose we've seen worse."

"Well, then. Have a look."

There was a squawk of hinge as the lid came up and over. Harry found himself staring into what had been the face of a man. Happily, the gore was clotted over with a thick dust that was scattered over his clothing and in his dark hair as well. Whatever money had been spent on his embalming and funeral had been wasted.

"You look disappointed, laddy buck. Or are you just ill?"

"I was expecting to find something else."

"And what besides a dead man would you expected to find in a dead man's coffin?"

"Gold."

"Gold?"

"I buried the gold at the San Miguel Church in Santa Fe, Harry Raines."

"Yes you did, Tantou, but that was a trifling amount. I was expecting a lot of gold—a chest of gold. If you will, a coffin full."

Gingerly, Leahy pushed the body up a little with his foot. "Nothing like that here."

Harry knelt at the side of the coffin, taking a deep breath. "Forgive me." He opened the man's coat, running his hands into the pockets, finding nothing. There were bloodstains on the shirt. Opening that garment, brushing away the insect life that was crawling thereon, Harry found dark circles of crusty blood in two places on the gray flesh of the man's hairless chest. He pondered this a moment.

"I want to roll him over."

"Why?"

"He was hit by more than the shotgun blast in the face."

They carefully turned the body over. "There. You see. Shot in the back."

Tantou lifted his head.

"What is it?" Harry asked.

"I thought I heard something, but maybe not."

There was a distant crack, sounding like a tree branch suddenly breaking. The bullet sang through the air between him and Tantou and struck the corpse with an explosion of dust and decaying flesh.

Chapter 22

HARRY flung himself to the head of the grave, using both the stone marker and the deceased's remains for cover. Leahy landed next to him. The two crowded together, as they might were they to share the same narrow bed. Two more bullets came their way, one striking the grave marker and causing the top of it to break off in a flurry of stone bits.

"Where's Tantou?" Harry asked.

Leahy quickly raised and lowered his head. "He's making a run for it. Fire at the bastards!"

"Where?"

"Doesn't matter. Shoot!"

Harry managed to pull one of his Navy Colts to hand without getting his arm shot off. Without looking where precisely, he stuck the pistol out beyond the grave marker and fired off three shots. Leahy, actually aiming his weapon from the other side, methodically emptied it.

"That'll take a while to reload," Harry said, as their

unseen foe replied with a small fusillade that kicked up several small clouds of dust.

"That's all right. Your Indian friend has made it."

"Made it where?"

"To the side of the church."

"He got me out of a tight spot like this farther down the Rio Grande."

"Let's hope he's still feeling that generous."

Another bullet struck the grave marker, making an odd, bell-like sound, but it remained intact. Harry finally worked up the courage to take a peek around the side. He was rewarded with two more rounds from the intruders, coming in close succession but hitting far apart, neither too near him.

"I saw them," he said. "I saw two puffs of smoke. By the church wall."

"Now there's a miracle worthy of this sacred ground. You're not wearing your specs."

More hostile bullets. Their adversary had changed aim. The rounds struck short now, hitting the unfortunate occupant of the grave again.

"I want one of these bullets," Harry said.

Another round, burning past Harry's ear, caused him to press against the stone tablet even more closely.

"Reach out and catch one," Leahy said, trying to load his revolver without exposing flesh and bone to probable harm.

"This is not foolishness. Doctor Gregg's science of ballistics. These bullets could match some that I have in my pockets."

"Maybe. Maybe not. One of these bastards is using a rifle. Big bore weapon. That's what knocked the top off the marker. You don't have one of those fifty calibers in your pocket, do you?"

"No."

"Let's tend to the business at hand."

Harry struggled to pull his pair of gold-rimmed spectacles from his pocket. Putting them in place, he leaned out quickly and fired at the place where he'd seen the puffs of smoke, ducking back before the shooters could respond. They did anyway.

"Do you know what's amusing about this?" Harry asked.

"That we're so convenient to a graveyard?"

"No. It's that I was hoping we'd be followed."

"Well, that's a foolishness I think I will forebear from sharing with Mr. Pinkerton—in the unexpected event of my ever again having an opportunity to do so."

"What I should have done is asked Tantou to keep watch on the trail while we dug up the grave."

"I wonder where he's gone."

"If we stopped talking, they might think we're dead and come up here to find out. We could shoot them as they drew near."

"I don't think they're that stupid, but I like the idea of stopping talking."

They lay still, listening. There was no wind. One of those large, dark birds was circling overhead, but made no sound. Harry leaned out the side of the grave marker one more time.

An echoing gunshot was the immediate result, the heavy round hitting the marker lower down and cracking it from one side to the other. A moment later, most of it fell down, hitting Harry squarely on his injured shoulder. He somehow kept himself from crying out. The chunk had hit

Leahy as well, but he had shoulder muscles harder even than rock.

Harry squinted up over the rims of his spectacles. The grave marker had been cut down to only about a foot high.

He realized then that he might actually be killed in this dusty, forsaken place, that his extremely interesting but as yet too brief life might end as soon as their assailants were able to get him in their sights. And it would be for no real reason. Brave and committed men had died in this canyon for what they believed in—good or bad. Such men were being slaughtered by the thousands back East, knowing at least that their sacrifice was part of a massive struggle for the future of the American nation. He and Leahy were about to give their all for nothing more significant than the satisfaction of a curiosity—and an infatuation with a beautiful woman. His curiosity, his infatuation.

There came three shots in quick succession and then a fourth—all slightly muffled and from a different position than the one Harry had located. He guessed it was from behind the church.

"It's Tantou!" he said.

Their foes replied in kind, and there was a considerable exchange. None of the rounds came their way. Leahy, now reloaded, nudged Harry. "Fire, boyo! Distract them!"

They did—Leahy nearly emptying his pistol again as Harry got off all of one shot.

Both now commenced reloading as echoes of the gun battle danced around the hillside. Harry had barely got one new round into his Colt's cylinder when shooting commenced again on the other side of the church. An instant later, there was an anguished cry. Then swearing—in Spanish.

More shots. Another cry. An interlude of quiet, then the sound of horses moving out over stony ground. Harry took a deep breath, then got to his feet. Tantou was standing by the far corner of the church, holding a rifle he had apparently retrieved from his own horse.

"I hit one," he said. "Twice."

HAVING saved their lives with his resourcefulness, Tantou attended to Harry's interest in the bullets imbedded in the dead man, going about the requisite posthumous surgery with the nonchalance of someone carving a chicken. After the one-sided gun battle, Harry was too rattled even to look at the corpse.

He accepted the recovered rounds with much gratitude, then went about digging up a few representative samples of the bullets fired at them in the just-ended encounter, dropping those from the dead body into one coat pocket and the remainder into another.

"You want to rebury him?" Tantou asked, touching the corpse with the toe of his boot.

Harry stopped to think upon this, then wondered why he was hesitating. "Of course. I'll do it. I'm greatly in your obligation as it is, sir."

Trying to be decorous, he gently used his own boot to shove the dead man back into his coffin, then carefully replaced the lid. It took only a short time to re-cover the grave with the sandy dirt. "Let's go back," he said.

"We've let them get away," said Tantou.

"Or they could be waiting in the canyon for us," Leahy said.

* * *

WITH Tantou in the lead, carrying his rifle across the pommel of his saddle, they descended the arroyo down to the canyon without incident. The Meti paused from time to time to study splotches of blood as he encountered them, concluding finally that the man he had shot was bleeding badly and might not have gotten very far.

"The abiding question here is whether his partner is still with him," said Leahy, "presuming there were only two of them."

"Only two," Tantou affirmed.

They turned into the canyon, heading west at a cautious walk. As they approached a narrow, steep-sided cut, Tantou of a sudden raised his rifle and came within a kitten's whisker of firing off a shot. But something stayed him, and after a moment, he lowered the weapon again. Harry looked to where the Meti had fixed his attention and saw a man on a height just ahead. He was standing and he appeared unarmed. As the three of them drew nearer him, he raised his hands.

Harry had his spectacles on. He saw that it was Anselmo. He pulled out one of his Colts. He hadn't the capability of putting a round within ten feet of the man at this distance, but the Mexican gentleman would not know that.

"Were you one of those shooting at us up at the graveyard?" Harry asked, raising his voice to be heard.

"I have come no farther than this, senor. I heard gunfire. As I came nearer, two men rode by fast. I wasn't sure if there were more, so I came up here to wait them out."

"You were following us."

"Yes."

"Why?

"Senorita Isabel wished to know what you would do here. I think she feared you would disturb her father's grave."

"Well, I must confess that fear was well placed," Harry said. "Would you please come down here, sir." He raised his Colt.

"No need for the pistol," Anselmo said. He started down the slope, stirring up considerable dust with the surprising swiftness of his descent.

"You said two riders went by," said Leahy, after Anselmo was standing among them. "Could you identify them?"

"That I could not, senor. They were heavily armed and rode fast."

Anselmo himself had a pistol in his belt—from the looks of it, a Confederate Leech and Rigdon revolver.

"May I see that firearm?" Harry asked.

The Mexican seemed resentful, but did as bidden. The barrel of the gun was cold, and it was fully loaded. The pistol fired .36 caliber rounds. Those Harry had dug out of the ground of the churchyard were of a much larger category.

Harry handed the weapon back. "Thank you, Anselmo. It's evident you were not up at the churchyard. But can you tell me why not—since you came here to see what we were about?"

"I heard the gunfire. I did not know if there were more shooters this way."

"There was only us," Leahy said.

Harry studied the man a moment, lighting a cigar. "Anselmo, I want you to come back with us."

"Come back where?"

"Back to the churchyard."

THE exhumation this time proceeded much more swiftly, owing largely to the poor job they had done of reburying the remains. Harry bade Anselmo to stand near while Leahy opened the lid.

"Is this Don Luis?" Harry asked.

"Yes. This is his grave."

"But is it him?"

Anselmo stepped closer, looking curiously at way the dead man's shirt had been cut asunder for the recovery of the bullet. "Yes." He took off his hat with one hand and made the sign of the cross with his other.

"He died badly."

"*Quién sabe?* He had enemies. Political enemies. These are very bad times in Santa Fe."

Harry looked to his two companions for counsel. They provided none. "We'll rebury him, then."

"For the second bloody time," Leahy said. "Let's not be doin' it a third."

RETURNING to the canyon, they proceeded warily, Tantou taking the lead. He stopped several times, pointing to the ground to note splashes and drippings of blood.

"Drying now," he said.

"What does that mean?" Harry asked.

"It means the sun's hot," Leahy suggested.

"Maybe they are now far ahead of us," Tantou said.

But he was wrong. A mile or more farther, the Meti

halted his horse and backed it close to the rocky face of the hillside. Harry and the rest of them followed his example—weapons drawn and hammers cocked. The sound Tantou had heard became clear to them as well—a trotting horse. In a moment, it came around a bend in the trail. Tantou lowered his rifle. The horse was riderless.

They found its owner a few hundred yards along, lying where he had apparently dropped from the saddle. He was face up and must have seen them coming, but raised not a hand to defend himself.

Tantou stopped his horse several feet distant, keeping to his saddle but holding his rifle at the ready. Harry dismounted and, pistol in hand, approached—glancing back once to make certain that Anselmo was still with them and within view and reach of Leahy and Tantou.

The man was young, with long dark hair, and no one Harry had ever looked upon before. He bore some resemblance to Roberto, however.

"Were you at the church up the canyon?" Harry asked.

The youth's face contorted with a cascading wave of pain. Then he opened his eyes, struggling to fix them on Harry. "Who are you?" he said, his voice heavily accented and barely audible.

"Harrison Raines. I'm an army scout." He refrained from saying which army. "Why were you shooting at us up there?"

"Grave . . . robbers." He spoke the two words as though each was a separate sentence.

The man tried to grin, but produced instead a horrible contortion of his mouth. Leahy came up and examined the man's wound, which appeared to be low in the right shoulder. The heavy caliber rifle bullet had made a thorough mess of everything there, raw bone sticking out of pulpy flesh that was oozing blood.

"There should be another wound," Tantou said. "Lower."

There was. The youth had been gut shot. In the two battles he had experienced, Harry had observed the queer phenomenon of wounded men clawing at their shirts and trouser tops to see where they'd been shot. If it was through the intestines, those who weren't screaming would simply lie back and await the inevitable.

It was a wonder this fellow had stayed so long aboard his horse.

"Who are you?" Harry asked.

The dark eyes stared back, but revealed nothing.

"That's Alejandro Martinez," Anselmo said. "He is the son of Don Carlos Martinez."

"Were you with your parents—*padres*—when they were killed?" Harry asked.

The man's lips moved and widened, but there were no words. Harry thought of the dying man with the sand-colored horse—Pablo Sanchez—and his last words.

He leaned very close now. "Are you part of San Jeronimo? What is that? Simply a church?"

"*Oro.*"

"What?" said Harry. "What did you say?"

"*Oro. La Liga de San Jeronimo. La liga de oro.*" He commenced making a choking, gurgling sound, which Harry suddenly realized was his last.

Harry stood up straight, backing away as a vile looking fluid began flowing from the man's mouth.

"I don't understand," he said to Anselmo. "What does it mean—*La Liga de San Jeronimo?*"

"It means, 'The League of San Jeronimo.' "

Harry thought upon this. "A secret league? A secret society?"

"Yes."

"Who are they?"

"I don't know. They are secret."

"Were they the ones who held me prisoner the other night?"

Anselmo hesitated, as though searching for a true but safe answer. "That is probable."

"Was Don Luis Alamaden a member?"

"I cannot say."

"Are you?"

The Mexican shook his head. "I was not in the fight at the church at San Jeronimo."

Leahy now stood over young Martinez. "What should we do with him? I'm bloody well not going to dig another grave."

"You don't want to bring back a horse without the man again," Tantou said.

"Let us tie him onto his horse." Harry turned to Anselmo. "Has he any family left?"

"*Sí.* His cousins. Isabel, Eduardo, and Roberto Almaden y Cortes."

MARTINEZ'S fellow shooter made no reappearance, though Tantou had feared he might do so before they got out of the canyon. When they at last emerged at the foot of the mesa near Johnson's Ranch, the Meti put his rifle back in its scabbard.

The road to Santa Fe beckoned, but Harry's eyes went to the smoldering wreckage of the Confederate wagon train. There was something in the trees that had caught his attention when they'd first passed this way.

"A brief digression, if you don't mind, gentlemen."

They followed him to the place he remembered. There, separate from the other vehicles, were the charred remains of a once elegant coach. It was incompletely burned. Inside the hanging door, strips of unburned satin lining were hanging from the ceiling. A red plush cushion on one of the seats was largely unharmed.

Occupying the rear facing seat was a partially burned chest, quite large, putting Harry in mind of the outline he remembered from Don Luis's study.

"Is this Don Luis's coach?" he asked Anselmo.

The other nodded. "I believe it is."

Harry climbed into the coach, careful not to soil his trousers on the ubiquitous char. The chest had a lock, but it had been shot open. Pulling forth the hasp of the hinge, Harry lifted the lid and peered within. Even in the shadows here, he could see that it contained pieces of iron and rocks.

Chapter 23

"I SEE that this time you brought the owner back with the horse," Colonel Weimers said. "That spares you a horse thief charge, but I don't know about murder."

The officer grinned to show he meant this was a joke. He had come out onto the gallery of the Palace of the Governors not a minute after Harry, drawing up with his little party out of the darkness, had asked to see him.

Not trusting the local judicial system Harry had brought the body of Alejandro Martinez to the Army instead of the county sheriff's office, as he supposed the law required. Weimers, despite his good humor, seemed to wish Harry hadn't.

"We found him in Glorieta Pass," Harry said. "He was alive then, but he didn't last long."

"Has he a name?" Weimers viewed the body thrown over the saddle with a look of small welcome.

Harry dismounted, not wanting to show the colonel discourtesy by remaining in the saddle and talking down to him. Leahy, Tantou, and Anselmo—as weary as Harry—remained on their mounts.

"There was some thought he might be Alejandro Martinez, the son of Don Carlos," Harry said. "But I've no idea."

"Have you perhaps an idea who might have shot him?"

Harry shook his head. "We think it might have been an Indian."

Weimers allowed himself a quick glance at Tantou. "I've no reports of Indians in that canyon. And we've got dispatch riders using that trail all the time."

"Well, sir," said Harry. "This man is dead from gunshots, and I didn't know what else to do with him other than bring him here."

"And here he certainly is. I'll have him taken down to the embalmer's. The sheriff will be curious about the matter, but I'll tell him the body was found on the trail by a scout. It's the truth, if not all of it."

"Thank you, Colonel. That will spare us some bother."

"What were you doing up there at Glorieta, Raines? Nothing going on there anymore. Or is there?"

Harry had prepared his answer. "I was taking a good look at the battlefield—for my report to Washington."

Weimers's good cheer showed signs of draining away. "I don't know what there is to report to Washington beyond what Chivington and Slough have said in the dispatches they've already sent on to Denver. Clear-cut Union victory. Tactics straight out of General Hannibal and the Punic Wars. And we're only territorial volunteers."

"The Carthaginians won all those battles," Harry said. "But they lost that war."

"So you read, do you, Mr. Raines? Well, it's not the Union Army that's losing this one."

Not in the West, perhaps. The East was quite another matter. But this was not a time for that discussion.

Weimers took a step back toward the door. "Will you join me for a drink?" Without waiting for an answer, he turned to the nearest soldier among those loitering on the gallery. "Sergeant, get a detail to take that dead man to an undertakers—and see if you can do it without a lot of people taking notice."

The enlisted man saluted and went to the burdened horse. Harry had already taken what he wanted—the dead Alejandro's pistol and rifle, which he had aboard his horse. He followed the colonel inside.

Weimers poured two small glasses brim full of whiskey, pushing Harry's to him. "Hard day, Mr. Raines?"

"A dusty one."

"Did you find Almaden's grave?"

"Yes I did. How did you know I was looking for it?"

"The Palace of the Governors gets all the rumors. There's one afoot that you're a detective Almaden's daughter has hired to find his killer."

"That is far from the case." Harry seated himself and took a sip of the whiskey. "But my associate, Mr. Leahy, he was once a police detective in Boston."

"Well, there you are. Always a kernel of truth lying around somewhere, if you look for it." He lighted a small cigar. "Did you find out anything, poking around the man's grave?"

"Its occupant is dead."

"And the dead man you brought in, did you find him in that graveyard?"

Harry shook his head. "Other end of the canyon. Colonel, do you know anything about a *Liga de San Jeronimo?*"

Weimers stroked his moustache. "San Jeronimo church

was the last holdout of the Mexicans in the Taos revolt. Long time ago. I know nothing of a league, though. Maybe it's a group of survivors from that scrap."

"Or believers."

"Believers in what?"

"A cause."

"A cause? Like the Secesh rebellion?"

"Like the abolition of slavery, or independence from the U.S. government. That's what those Taos rebels at the San Jeronimo church were fighting for."

"Too much of that kind of cause going around these days."

An awkward silence followed.

"Colonel, may I see that list of Confederate sympathizers again?"

Weimers reached into an upper drawer of his desk. *"Suspected* sympathizers." He handed it over.

"Did you not notice something strange here?" Harry held the paper for him to see.

The colonel was puzzled. "A list of names. Many prominent people of the town, or so I'm told. You see what's written at the top? 'Friends of the Rebellion.' Couldn't be more obvious."

"All of them but one are Mexican," Harry said. "The only Anglo is the lady from New Orleans, who proclaims her Southern passions quite openly."

"Yes, she does. My general would like to lock her up as a Southern agent—except a real agent wouldn't be so damned fool obvious about her politics."

"But why no other Anglos on this list? Half the people in my hotel would huzzah Jeff Davis if he rode into town. Why aren't their names here?"

Weimers shrugged. "It is curious, ain't it? But this list was drawn up by Major Pyron himself—the Confederate commander here. Not us. We found it in this very desk. Another whiskey?"

Harry stood up. "No, thank you, sir. I must attend to business."

"Well, you do that. But before you leave town, I do hope you will explain to me just what this 'business' of yours is really all about."

OUTSIDE, the dead man and his horse had been taken away. Leahy, still on his mount, was all alone.

"Where is Anselmo?" Harry asked.

"He left."

"How is that?"

"He wished to go."

"Damn it," muttered Harry.

"Damn it, indeed, laddy buck," said Leahy. "You left no instruction to keep him. And you've got no authority to be instructing me, anyhow. I outrank you, Raines—need I remind?"

"And Tantou?"

"After Anselmo left, he left, too."

"To follow him?"

"Didn't say. Just disappeared."

"Sorry, Joseph. I should have said something. I am awful weary from this day." He thought of the food and drink in the cantina—and his soft bed—as he climbed aboard One-Eye.

"Where are you going?" Leahy asked.

Harry looked across the plaza to his hotel. He could not

tell at this distance whether there was a light on in his room or not.

"To the Almaden house."

LEAVING their horses in the livery stable near their hotel, they walked to the Almaden residence, keeping to the darkest shadows as much as possible. There were creatures in the street, loose chickens and pigs, mostly, and the occasional rat. Here and there, humans skulked along in the dark as well.

The front door of the house was locked. Harry rapped the knocker twice, then again more loudly. Dogs started barking up and down the street, but there was no other response. They moved down to the door in the wall that led to the courtyard. That was barred.

"I need to get into this house," Harry said to Leahy.

"Then we'll have to go over this wall."

"How?"

"Harry, m'lad. Don't be unimaginative."

Positioning Harry close to the wall, the Irishman carefully put his hands on Harry's shoulders. An instant later, he vaulted onto Harry's shoulders, then thrust himself up onto the top, leaving Harry with a feeling of immense physical relief.

"What do you see?" Harry asked.

"Shhhh," said Leahy. Kneeling, he reached down and took Harry's forearm in a steely grip. "Ready?"

"Yes."

He seemed to rise as though shot from a cannon. Leahy pulled him so forcefully that Harry wrenched a knee against the wall and then rolled completely over it, falling noisily and painfully into a thorny bush on the other side.

Every dog in the city seemed now to be taking note of them. Leahy dropped effortlessly to the ground beside him, helping him to his feet.

"Why didn't you just unbar the door?" Harry asked, with a grunt.

"Wasn't imaginative enough," the Irishman said.

A side door of the kitchen, near the courtyard cistern, proved to be unlocked. Moving inside, they went to the hall, shrinking back as they glimpsed Lucia, the serving maid, standing barefoot at the far end, bearing a stack of sheets or blankets. She proceeded up the stairs without noticing them.

"What do you want to do in here?" Leahy asked.

"Talk to Isabel. Go through Don Luis's desk again. Find Anselmo. Not find Roberto."

Weapons drawn, they went up the front stairs. Neither was wearing spurs, and their ascent was quiet.

Leahy paused on the landing. "Which room was Roberto in?"

"I've no idea."

"Anselmo?"

"I don't know."

"We'll try them one by one."

They went through four bedrooms in quick succession, finding each empty. The last, the source of Harry's fondest recent memories, was unoccupied, too. Alas.

Harry slumped on the edge of the bed. "She's gone."

"She goes where she will."

"Leaving no word."

Leahy put his revolver into his belt. "I think we should leave, with or without word."

"No. I want to look through Don Luis's study."

"What for?"

"For whatever's there. It's also time I introduced you to the science of ballistics."

THE maid did see them this time, just as they were coming down the stairs. She said nothing, moving toward the rear of the house as though they were merely house guests.

There was an oil lamp on Don Luis's desk, which Harry quickly lighted, seating himself carefully in the dead man's chair. Leahy, weary in mind and spirit, as he seldom seemed in body, dropped into a large, rug-draped one by the fireplace, stretching out his legs.

Harry went to work. Finding pencil and paper, he carefully emptied his pockets of the various pistol and rifle rounds he'd recovered, including several from Alejandro Martinez's firearms. Holding each up to the lamp light and using the pencil as a measure, he made a few notations, then leaned back in his chair.

"I have come to a conclusion," he said, with a sigh.

"I hope it has to do with sleep, or our return to the East."

"No, it does not."

Another yawn. "Well, then, out with it."

"What might prompt a man to kill his own father?"

"A hundred things. It was not an uncommon crime in the city of Boston when I was a police officer."

Harry stared up at the ceiling for a long moment, then started pulling out desk drawers, reexamining things he'd looked at before and finding a few papers he'd not noticed. He unfolded one that proved to be a drawing of some sort—a landscape. Very primitive.

"I don't suppose you are well acquainted with ancient Indian cultures?" he asked.

Leahy appeared to be nearly asleep. "Nothing beyond Squanto and the Massachusetts Bay Colony."

"Perhaps we can add to your education, then, before we depart this place." Harry pocketed the map. When he looked to Leahy again, the man was fully alert.

"What is it?" Harry asked, quietly.

"Someone has come into the house."

Chapter 24

BEFORE either could move from their chairs, the study door opened and the maid Lucia stepped in, followed by a long-barreled revolver pointed at her head, and then the stark, silent figure of Tantou. He closed the door behind him, keeping his revolver in place. It was then that Harry noticed the large sack in his hand.

"Where have you been?" Harry asked.

"It is bad for you out there," said the Meti. "There are Spanish—Mexicans—looking for you all over town."

"How do you know that?"

"There was one in the hotel room. Others outside."

"They didn't go after you?"

"They didn't see me."

The girl moved away from the gun and closer to Harry. She then spoke a few angry words in Spanish, her eyes flashing sentiments even stronger.

Tantou lowered the pistol.

"Did you understand any of that?" Harry asked the others.

"She said she hasn't bothered us—and won't," Leahy said. "She doesn't care that we're here."

"That can't be right."

More words—several sentences. The young woman smoothed her skirt and waited, still looking annoyed.

"She said Anselmo told her we were coming, and to welcome us and give us food."

"She hasn't given us a crumb. And when I knocked on the door she didn't answer it."

Leahy spoke to her now in his poor Portuguese, but she did not appear to understand. When she spoke again, it was to Harry.

"Anselmo say you sleep here," she said, her English surprising and worrying him. What had he said that she might have heard?

"Tonight?" said Tantou. *"Esta noche?"*

"Sí. Like before."

"Where is Senorita Almaden?" Harry asked.

The girl shrugged, then looked down at her pretty feet.

"And Anselmo?"

The response was much the same.

"Roberto?"

The mention of that name seemed to startle her. She shook her head vigorously.

Harry rubbed his chin. He needed a shave—and wanted one.

"I don't want to sleep here, Harry Raines," said Tantou.

"I don't, either, Jack. Not in the present circumstance. But I don't think anyone will be looking for us here."

"That won't keep them from finding us if they do come here."

"Hambre?" asked the maid.

"What man?" Harry asked.

"Not *hombre*," said Leahy. "*Hambre*. She's asking if we're hungry."

"I suppose we are," Harry said. He smiled at her and nodded and then gestured to the door.

"What's in the bag?" Harry asked Tantou.

The Meti held it up. "You do not recognize it?"

"No."

"It's the gold we took from that palomino horse. I went down to the San Miguel church and dug it up again."

"Who told you to do that?"

"I thought maybe we leave Santa Fe now."

Harry frowned. "I haven't finished here."

"I think you're only wasting time, laddy buck," said Leahy. "Yours, ours, and the federal government's. We've lost a day now with that jaunt up the canyon and back. Instead of Senor Almaden's killer, you only found more dead bodies—and came close to adding us to the tally. There's this Mexican cult of Thugee out there looking to put an end to you—and our duty to Mr. Pinkerton and the Union goes begging. We're weeks from a ship or a telegraph. And you're squandering the days like a spend-thrift does dollars."

"Something may have happened to her."

"Something seems to have happened to her whole bloody family. But I don't view that as our concern any-more—no matter how obliged the army is to her father."

Harry took out the odd, primitive drawing he had taken from the desk, certain now that it was a map. "I can't give either of you gentlemen orders—or make demands on you. But if you would please indulge me, I'd like to devote another day to this matter."

"Harry . . ."

"Just one day. And we won't be spending it in Santa Fe."

Leahy sighed in resignation.

"Where do we go?" Tantou asked.

Harry rose. "Before we do anything, may I see that sack of gold again?"

"It is all there, Harry Raines. I am no thief."

"I know that. Please."

Tantou set the bag on the desk, loosening the tie. Harry opened it wider, taking out a few pieces and holding them to the light.

"I'd paid no attention to the fact," he said, "but these are minted twenty dollar gold pieces. Federal specie. Not Spanish dollars. Not pesos. Not gold dust or nuggets."

"This is federal territory."

"Yes, but what would someone like Pablo Sanchez be doing with it? An agent of the Mexican government. Where'd he get it?"

"I'm tiring of these riddles, Harry."

"I think the answer is Texas."

"He was riding toward Texas."

"No. He was riding toward Mexico."

Leahy stood up. "Raines, you're either as tired as I am or suffering from your too-frequent imbibing of spiritous liquors. Go find a bed and we can conclude this conversation more clearly in the morning—on our way out of town. On our way to Denver."

"Can't yet." Harry turned to Tantou. "Where did you have this gold buried at the church? By the wall, did you say?"

"By the wall. Inside the wall. The little burying ground."

"Bloody hell," said Leahy. "Another cemetery."

"Did you mark the place in any way?"

"It's by a grave marker. A big one, where a priest is buried."

Harry retied the sack then handed it back to the Meti. "I'd like you to put it back there."

Tantou simply stared. For a moment, Harry feared the man would turn on his heel and walk out of the house and vanish from their lives forever.

"Why?" he said.

"Because I'm going to arrange to have some people try to dig it up again."

"What people?"

"That's what I want to find out."

"Raines . . ."

"I ask this as a favor—which I will repay tenfold. Please rebury this at the Church of San Miguel and then wait there for me. I would be most obliged to you, Joseph, if you would assist us."

"Where are you going in the meantime?"

"I'm going to call upon a lady."

"Raines, if I relate just half of this lunacy to Pinkerton, he's going to have you locked up in the Dry Tortugas."

The maid appeared in the doorway, bearing a tray of food.

"Muchas gracias," Harry said. "But we must go."

"No. You must stay. Anselmo say so." She set down the tray, and stood with hands on hips.

"We'll return," Harry said, lying.

*   *   *

HE and Leahy lay on the hard, cold ground behind a grave perhaps twenty feet from the dead priest's. Tantou stretched out prone in the manner of a cat atop the wall, a position giving him a view of both the street and the gateway to the churchyard and one Harry figured to be even less comfortable than his own.

They had been there more than an hour.

"What did you tell her?" Leahy asked quietly.

"Madame Beignet?"

"That is where you went, isn't it?"

"She took some waking."

"You just whispered where the gold could be found into her ear and then kissed her good-bye?"

"I told her I was leaving Santa Fe to return to the Confederacy. I said that to prove my loyalty to the cause I would tell her where you hid the gold."

"She appears not to have believed you."

"Or she was not believed."

"We could be here all bloody night."

"No. I don't think so."

Tantou struck the wall twice with something hard, possibly the handle of his knife. Then he raised his hand.

"Where did you leave the horses?" Harry whispered.

"In an empty house just down the street."

"Inside the house?"

"No one will notice them there."

Tantou rapped again, and they ceased talking. Harry shifted himself for a better view of the churchyard entrance, just as a dark shape appeared in it. It vanished, then another appeared in its place, and then another after that.

Harry watched them flit along the wall, hearing a quick exchange in Spanish he could not quite make out. For a moment, he feared that one of them might be Madame Beignet, a factor he had not calculated upon.

He took out one of his Navy Colts, planning to use the butt end to accomplish his ends here. Leahy quickly did the same. Tantou was all but one with his wall.

One of the shadowy figures located the dead priest's grave, then called the others to it. They studied the marker, lighting a match to make certain, then blew it out and turned their attention to the churchyard wall. Tantou had piled the dirt loose and high, so there'd be no mistaking the cache.

The three discovered it quickly. While two of them knelt and began to dig with knives, the other went to stand sentry at the churchyard gate. Harry had hoped to catch all three together. He'd have to leave the third to Tantou.

Leahy gripped Harry's shoulder, nodding to the two diggers, then started forward on hands and knees at the slow, keeping boots from dragging on the ground and advancing with no sound. Harry tried to emulate him as closely as possible.

They struck almost in unison, hitting their prey with the pistols at the back of their heads. Harry was careful not to swing so hard that he might kill the poor devil he'd targeted, but that proved too gentle. The man—it was definitely not Madame Beignet—recovered from the blow and tried to grab hold of Harry's arm, leaving Harry no choice but to whack at the fellow's skull again. He went down with a moan.

There were running footsteps. The third intruder was returning from the gateway, fast, with something in his hand that undoubtedly was a pistol. An instant later, Tantou rose like some great predatory bird and leaped down on him, sending him rolling. There was a thump, and everything went still.

"You all right, Jack?" Harry asked.

The Indian stood. "Yes."

"Are they all alive? We're in big trouble if we've killed anyone."

"Our two are breathing," Leahy said.

"This one lives," said Tantou. "He is lucky."

"I need to look at their faces," Harry said. "Then we go."

He went from one to another, striking matches, coming back to the one he had felled.

"You recognize any of them?" Leahy asked.

"Yes. One of them," Harry replied.

"This Roberto fellow?"

"No. He's not here. The man's name is Emiliano Vasquez."

"So?"

"So I was right. Let's be off."

THEY rode out of town at a gallop, taking two Union army sentries by surprise. A shot was fired, going wide.

Pulling up at the first crossroads, Harry looked back to see if there was pursuit.

"We're clear of them," Leahy said. "Well clear."

"They'll know who we were, but not where we'll go."

"You don't want to go back?" Tantou asked.

"No. No reason now."

"We sleep in the desert?"

"Yes." Harry swore. "Oh no."

"What's wrong now?" Leahy asked.

"We forgot the gold."

"Laddy, if you think we're . . ."

"The gold is tied to my saddle, Harry Raines," said Tantou.

"What did you bury then?"

"Nothing."

Moving out at a trot, they headed north under a cold and starry sky.

Chapter 25

POSSESSED of more education than was usual among Southern gentlemen, Harry had some small notion of history—Napoleon, the England of Shakespeare and Walter Scott, the Romans, the Greeks, the ancient Persians.

None of this prepared him for the overwhelming sense of ages past that overcame him as he and his two companions descended the trail that took them into the steep-sided, flat-bottomed Frijoles Canyon.

The high stone cliffs, rising from either side of a tree-lined meandering stream, embraced a natural amphitheater that seemed intended for the worship of the heavens. But what awed him so had not to do with nature but with man. There were phenomenal alterations made upon the lower face of the cliff, the work of laboring human hands millennia before.

At the widest place on the valley floor, arranged in a wide circle, were the foundation walls and ruins of what must have been an entire community—a large kiva at one corner serving as the predominant structure. Farther up the canyon, ascending four and five stories up the cliff, were row upon row of caves and holes carved deeply into the stone. They looked back at him as might a multitude of eyes in a gigantic skull.

All this had been the dwelling place of a people who had come into this region ten thousand years or more before. The morning wind, blowing across the spectral apertures, produced a sound not unlike the wailing of their lost souls. Despite the heat, Harry shivered.

"What do you call them, Tantou? Anastazi?"

"Anasazi," the Meti corrected. "It's the Navajo word for them. I don't know what they called themselves."

"This place gives me a queer feeling. It's as though they were still here."

"No, Harry Raines. They been gone for hundreds of years. No one knows why. Wars, maybe. Or sickness."

"Someone's still here," Leahy said.

They had come to a narrow point in the canyon where a grove of trees grew in a bunch to one side of the stream. Moving closer, Harry noticed a horse tied to a branch. Then he saw a second. They were saddled. Spanish saddles.

Raising his hand to halt all further conversation, Harry slowly moved forward. Crossing the little stream and proceeding into the grove, he stopped under the cover of a broad-branched tree.

Two horses only—tied to brush but at some distance from one another. Harry urged One-Eye a little nearer, pausing now to look up and down the canyon. No other animal—or human—in sight in either direction.

Leahy came up alongside him. He had his pistol out.

"Only two," Harry said. "I was expecting more."

"The other brother, too, maybe?"

"Eduardo? Possibly. Maybe his sister."

"That's not expecting, boyo. That's wishing."

Tantou drew up on Harry's other side.

"How far does this canyon go, do you think?" Harry asked.

"The way this stream runs—flat and fast—I would say far."

"Their horses are here, so they must be near."

Tantou pointed up the cliff face. "There," he said. "That cave."

"Which cave? How can you tell?" Harry had left his spectacles in their pocket case.

"There. The one with the ladder."

Harry transferred his eyeglasses to a more useful place. Tantou was indicating a very large cave, three tiers above the canyon floor, the ladder extending from it down to near a smaller cave on the tier just beneath.

"How does one get up there?" Harry wondered aloud.

"You use the ladder," Tantou said. "But you start at the bottom. Then you pull it up after you."

"They must be in there," Leahy said.

"There is, alas, only one way to find out."

BACKTRACKING downstream, Tantou found a wide ravine running back into the canyon wall. Dismounting, he clambered up a steep fall of rock, then used handholds to climb from there up a cleft in the cliff face that became a narrow crevice. At its top was the beginning of a ledge that led back to the area of the caves. Less nimbly, Harry followed Tantou along it, with the agile Leahy bringing up the rear.

It took them near to half an hour to traverse the wall

and reach the place with the ladder. Twice Harry came close to falling and would have done so had Leahy not grabbed hold of him in time and held him up.

There was very little room for them on the ledge. The ladder, nearly vertical, had so little purchase, Harry wouldn't have taken ten thousand dollars to climb it.

But he had to. Now, and for nothing—the only prize the conclusion of this long pursuit.

"Can you hold this steady for me?" he asked, in a whisper.

"I'll go up," Tantou whispered back.

"No. I'll do it. You might shoot her."

"She's not here, Harry. She wouldn't come to a place like this."

Harry put a foot to a cross piece. The ladder seemed so old it might have been constructed by the original people here.

His friends somehow kept it from wobbling. Harry took his time, not moving one foot until the other was firmly planted. Nearing the top, he reached to take a revolver from his belt, making the mistake of looking down. He almost toppled backward then and there.

Returning the weapon to its place—holding fast to the ladder—he took a deep breath, then lifted his eyes to the ledge above again. Two more steps and he was able to see into the shadowy depth of the cave, noting a table-like stone ledge covered by a blanket. He was able to make out a large woven basket, and two wine bottles.

Two steps more and he was on the ledge and into the cave, pistol held firmly with the hammer cocked. Waiting a moment for his eyes to adjust to the gloom, he proceeded deeper within, surprised to find a turning at the rear and a square-walled chamber beyond. The breeze blew cool here. He felt as though he had entered a tomb.

What appeared to be clothing was scattered on the hard floor, and there were more wine bottles and baskets containing the remnants of meals. A small rodent crawled out of one, stood on hind legs a moment with a chunk of some foodstuff in its mouth, then skittered away. It was then that Harry heard the groan.

"COME up," said Harry, leaning out over the ledge. "Come up quick."

"Is anyone in there?" Leahy asked, ascending the ladder at twice the speed Harry had.

"Yes."

"Not the lady."

"No. It's Anselmo."

The Mexican had been bound, hand and foot, and left on the floor. Whoever had done that had perpetrated other unkindnesses upon the poor man. Anselmo had a cut beside one eye and a bruise on the opposite cheek. His lip was swollen and there were scratch marks along the right side of his neck.

He spoke not a word, even as they released him from his bonds and propped him up against the cave wall. Leahy had brought his canteen up with him, slung over his shoulder. Anselmo accepted a few swallows gratefully, his eyes moving from one to another of them, settling finally on Harry.

"You should not have come, senor," he said, wiping his mouth with a hand that appeared to have been stepped on a few times. "You're in danger here. He's not far. He'll come back."

"Who?" Harry looked around the empty chamber.

"Roberto."

"Roberto. Not Eduardo?"

The Mexican rubbed the bruise on his face. "Roberto. I have reason to remember."

"He did this to you? Why?"

Anselmo took another swallow of water. "You were supposed to stay at Don Luis's house in Santa Fe. You would have been safe there. Why did you come?"

"The town was full of people after our scalps. People from the *Liga de San Jeronimo*."

"What do you know about the *Liga de San Jeronimo*?" Anselmo asked.

"Enough, I think. Where is she?"

"Where is who?"

Harry liked the man, but his disingenuousness could be an irritant.

"Isabel. I believe she left Santa Fe to come here, as did you. Now where is she? In one of these caves?"

"I speak the truth, senor Raines. I do not know where she is. What I do know is where her brother Roberto is, which is very near. You were foolish to come here."

"He has a point, laddy buck," said Leahy. "As the lady is not present, why do we not move on? It's a long way we have to travel just to get on the road to Denver."

Tantou moved back to the entrance of the cave and then inched onto the outside ledge, looking to the right, the left, up high, and down below.

"No one," he said.

"Keep watch. If Roberto shows himself, give us a shout."

Anselmo shook his head. "Not out there." With some effort, he pointed to the rear of the cave. "These chambers are connected. There's a passage back there that leads to the next cave. You can move through them, right through the rock, one to the other, for a long way. But he will come back, because he left the ladder here, and there's no other way to get back down."

Leahy went to the rear of the next chamber, finding the entrance to a neighboring cave up near the ceiling. "I see it," he said. "It's a wee space." He took out his revolver and sat on the blanket-covered stone shelf just below the opening, waiting.

"Now we're prepared on both flanks," Harry said, pleasantly. "This affords us an opportunity for conversation, Anselmo—however brief."

Anselmo stretched out his legs, wincing. "Very well. Some wine, *por favor*. There are some bottles back there."

Harry went to fetch one. "This cave is certainly well provisioned. Who arranged for that?" He pulled the cork. There were no glasses, so he handed the bottle to Anselmo as it was.

"This was all here when I came," the other said, after taking a long drink. "Someone has been staying here."

Harry settled onto the cave floor next to him, leaning back against the cave wall and lighting a small cigar. His offer of one to Anselmo was declined.

"This is an excellent hiding place—as well as redoubt," Harry said, "as must have occurred to the original occupants."

"Maybe not so good. You found it."

"I had a general idea where it might be. I found a sort of map in Don Luis's desk. It was Tantou who did the tracking. This is a man who could track an ant across glass."

"You are fortunate in your companions, senor. As I have not been."

Harry let a slow, billowing cloud of fragrant smoke escape his lips.

"Why did you come?" Anselmo asked. "What do you want of me?"

"Nothing of you. I'm looking for Isabel. And for gold."

"You will find neither."

"We have a sack of the gold with us, which we found among the possessions of Senor Pablo Sanchez, the now-deceased gentleman from Mexico. But I am sure this is only a very small portion of the total. A thousand dollars at most. What I'm seeking is many thousands, enough gold to arm and supply a small army."

"So you're here out of greed, like all the rest. I should have expected this."

"You misjudge me, sir. I am here in my capacity as a Union Army scout."

The Mexican took a long draught of the wine, offering the bottle finally to Harry, who nodded thanks and drank.

"This is from Don Luis's cellar, isn't it?" he asked. "I believe I recognize it from our pleasant dinner." He drank again. "Yes. The very same."

"You are a man of some discernment. Like Don Luis."

"You continue to lead me off into other subjects, Anselmo."

"Like the wine, senor, conversation is good for the soul."

"Then let us turn back to the subject that interests me—Isabel, and gold. Where are they?"

Anselmo gestured to the emptiness of the cave. "There is none here. None in this canyon."

"At Glorieta and down along the Rio Grande, I have come upon chests large enough to contain a great fortune in gold, Anselmo. One, as you saw, was in the wreck of Don Luis's coach. But instead of gold, they were filled with rock and iron. But someone must have thought they contained gold. People were killed for it. And now Roberto has come here, looking for gold. Mine is not an unreasonable surmise."

"She told me to tell you she was sorry."

"Isabel?"

"Yes. She was sorry she had to leave you the way she did. But I think she would be sorry to find you here, looking for gold where there is none."

"Is that all she said? She was sorry?"

"I think so."

"She said nothing more about me? She left no message."

"No."

"Anselmo, you do know where she is, don't you?"

"I do not. I swear on my mother's grave."

"Harry!" It was Leahy, calling from the rear chamber. "You're wasting our time. Let's go find this damned Roberto, take him back to Santa Fe, and be on our way."

"He is right, Harry Raines," said Tantou.

"We have time," Harry said. "It's a very nice day."

A gunshot. A bullet smacked into the cave wall back near Leahy, echoing oddly and endlessly through the hollowed cliff.

"Are you all right?" Harry asked.

"Just some bloody damned rock splinters. I am fine." He presented his own pistol and let off a shot.

None came in reply.

"Did you hit him?" Harry asked.

"No. He's smart, this one. He's just waiting."

Tantou ran back to the little passage, returning soon. He came back to Harry, shaking his head.

"We can't go through there now. He'd kill us quick. But he can't come through this way, either."

"Can you tell precisely where he is?"

"Right in the next cave, I expect. If we go after him along the ledge, he can hit us there, too."

"But he can't be in both places at once—by the passage and by the front."

"He might as well be in both places, Harry Raines, because we don't know which place he's in. He is trapped. We are trapped."

"We have the ladder," Harry said. "Without it, he can't get down. Can't get to the horses."

"As long as he's there, we can't either," said Tantou. He moved back to the cave front, taking a quick look to the side.

Another shot, this one from Leahy, deafening in this enclosure. "Thought I saw him move."

Anselmo got unsteadily to his feet, rubbing his shin. "Roberto is impatient." He pointed to the bruise on his face. "He is very frustrated. Maybe he will do something stupid and we can take advantage."

As if to underscore that remark, another shot came their way, banging about the cave in a wild ricochet that left it finally spinning on the floor.

"Bloody brilliant idea, you're getting us trapped in here, Harry," said Leahy. "You ought to be a Union army general."

When the bullet ceased its rotations, Harry knelt and tried to pick it up, dropping it at once because it was so hot.

Tantou reached and gathered it up for him, rubbing it against his pants leg and then handing it to Harry.

While they were so engaged, Roberto appeared at the entrance to the cave. He had just one weapon, a large revolver pointed at Harry. He stood there calmly, if a little wild eyed, confident he had gained the upper hand, but not knowing quite how to play it.

"Move together," he said. "All of you."

Leahy was reluctant, but Harry, Tantou, and Anselmo did as bidden.

Roberto came a step closer, but not within reach of any of them. As with his pistol, his attention was fixed on Harry.

"What you have done with my sister?" he asked.

"I have done nothing with her. I am looking for her, just like you."

Roberto came yet closer. He had not cleansed his teeth. "What has happened to my father's gold?"

"Your father's gold?"

Yet another gunshot ruptured the quiet of the cave, the bullet striking the ceiling just inside the cave opening. None of them had fired. It had come from outside.

Harry heard someone call out, then do so again. Roberto kept his pistol on them, but moved to the side of the cave. Looking toward the source of sounds, he shouted a long string of Spanish words, presumably curses, out into the canyon. Then he fired his pistol—twice—aiming below.

In response, seemingly a hundred firearms opened up on them, the bullets striking the cliff wall like rain. Harry and the others followed Roberto's example and moved hastily away from the opening.

"It is unusual to have so many people come to this canyon," Anselmo said.

Chapter 26

"**I** should have brought my rifle," said Tantou, abjectly. "It is with my horse. Useless."

The thought of climbing up that crude ladder with such an unwieldy weapon made Harry dizzy.

"There are too many guns down there," Anselmo said. "Your rifle would do little good."

"Tantou's an excellent shot," Harry said. "He'd discourage them a little."

"But the result in the end would be the same," said Anselmo.

"Who are those people, and why are they so bloody mad at us?" Leahy asked, crouching near the cave opening but out of the line of fire.

Anselmo directed his answer to Harry. "You spoke of the *Liga de San Jeronimo*. There they are."

"They're crazy," Roberto said. "They dream of the Old Mexico."

There was more gunfire—loud, closer, and more accurate.

One bullet struck just above Leahy's head. Swearing, he edged back.

"We've got to do something, boyo." He began to reload his revolver.

Harry took out his pocket watch. It was getting late in the day. "I'll grant you this is not the best place to pass the night."

There was more fire, the rounds chipping away at the ceiling. Dropping to the floor, Harry crept up to the edge of the ledge. Spectacles still in place, he lifted his head for perhaps two seconds to make a swift reconnaissance before anyone could take careful aim at him.

He'd seen only three figures in the grove below, though there were doubtless many more. Two had been standing by trees, but not behind them. Another was in the open by the creek. Very overconfident.

He'd seen something else—mostly hidden but unmistakable. A large open carriage.

"I'll talk to them," Harry said.

"What?"

"A parley. A truce."

"What'll that accomplish?"

"I don't know. Find out what they want. Figure out how many are down there."

"They'll just shoot you down if you show yourself," Roberto said.

Remaining in the shadows, Tantou peered out at the canyon, making a quick assessment.

"It's a good idea, Harry Raines. While you parley, the rest of us can go through that passage into the next cave."

"Maybe we can put some enfilade fire down on them

from there," Leahy said. "Discourage 'em even more."

"I'll go through first," Tantou said. "Find a place where I can give you covering fire."

"With only your pistol?"

"I am pretty damn good."

Without further word, he went to the rear, and in a moment, disappeared, quietly.

"Let's go," Leahy said to the others.

Only Roberto followed.

"I am a poor fit," Anselmo said. "And can only hobble besides. I'll stay here with Senor Raines."

Harry needed something white. It occurred to him there was only his shirt. It was badly soiled, but he thought it would suffice.

He pulled off his coat and waistcoat, then removed the shirt, ripping it slightly. Crawling to the cave opening again, he waited. "Let me know when they're through the passage," he said to Anselmo.

"I am sure the Indian is there now."

Inching forward, Harry swung the shirt in the air. It attracted a few bullets, as it might flies, but nothing hit his hand or arm.

Finally, there was quiet.

"I want to speak to Madame Beignet!" he shouted.

This caused some consternation. "What makes you think she is here?"

"I saw her carriage."

"No you did not."

"It is the only barouche in Santa Fe," Harry replied. "Get her, so we can put an end to this before somebody gets killed."

It occurred to him that somebody getting killed was the main reason these people had come.

There was some discourse in Spanish, then, "She won't go up there."

"I don't blame her. But she doesn't have to. Just to the base of the cliff."

More conversation. "Okay. You wait."

Harry lay there while they deliberated. Looking right along the cliff, he saw Tantou's head and shoulder just behind a small crooked rock by a cave opening perhaps a hundred feet distant.

"She wants to know who is with you, senor."

"Only my two friends."

"No, you have five horses."

"Tell him I am here," Anselmo said.

Harry nodded. "Anselmo Sabio is here."

"Who else from the Almaden family?"

"No more answers till I talk to her." He pulled himself back from view.

A few minutes later, he heard his name called. "Madame Beignet?"

"Yes. What do you want?"

Holding his white shirt, Harry crept out onto the ledge again. The stone on the cave floor had been cold against his bare chest, but out in the sun he was warmed.

She crossed Frijoles Creek in her long dark dress and stood on hard ground about thirty or forty feet below him, holding a parasol. Two well-armed Mexicans, one bearing a rifle, stood protectively to either side of her. He recognized the man on the left as Emiliano Vasquez. He had a bandage around his head and appeared to be in a disagreeable mood.

"*Bonjour*, madame," he said. "How did you find us?"

"We followed you from the church. You left a wide track. What do you want to speak to me about?"

"I want to know what you want from us. So that I might give it to you and you can let us go."

"Very well, monsieur. These people want their gold back, and they want Roberto."

"Why Roberto?"

"Because they think he and his brother Eduardo murdered Don Carlos Martinez and his wife to steal this gold."

"How do they know it wasn't Alejandro Martinez who did it?"

"They don't know, but Alejandro is dead and they cannot talk to him. Roberto is not yet dead."

"But if he stole the gold, why would he come here looking for it."

"I don't know. They intend to ask him."

"And Pablo Sanchez? What about his murder?"

"They care nothing about him."

"The sack of gold coins he was carrying. It's in my saddlebags. I'll let you take it if you let us go."

"We have already taken it, monsieur. It belongs to them."

She tilted back her parasol. He could see the displeasure and impatience in her face.

"*Alors*, monsieur. Let us conclude."

"Well, we haven't any gold."

"*Je ne suis pas une imbecile, monsieur.* You did not come out here to look at old Indian dwellings."

As Madame Beignet could not from where she stood, Harry could see from his elevated vantage all the way to the head of the canyon, and the track that led down into it. There was rising dust.

"You wear black, madame. Are you still grieving for Don Luis de Almaden, or did you have a hand in what happened to him?"

"Don Luis was a fool. A misguided, ridiculous idealist. He believed in the wrong cause."

"Like many a Confederate sympathizer I could name." Harry glanced quickly to the entrance of the next cave. Roberto was showing too much of himself.

"You are no Confederate, monsieur."

"Thank you for the compliment."

"I am tired of talking. Have you their gold?"

"When you say, *their* gold, madame, don't you mean *your* gold? Didn't you give it to them, in the care of Don Luis?"

"You are wasting our time. Do you have the gold or not?

"If we had found it, we would not still be here." Harry could hear the sound of the approaching horses now. He wondered if she could.

"I do not believe you. Tell us where it is and give us Roberto, and we will let you go."

"You don't fear we would go straight to the Union Army?"

She began backing away. "You vex me, sir."

Vasquez took a step closer to the cliff. "You will go nowhere, senor. This is our country here. You cannot escape us."

A gunshot. Harry saw Vasquez begin to crumple. Madame Beignet turned and ran, and then she went down. To the right, Harry saw someone tumble out of the cave. By then the air in front of him was full of zinging bullets. Anselmo was pulling him back.

They retreated to the chamber behind the cave. Anselmo picked up a bottle of wine, seated himself on the ledge, and took a long drink.

"There were riders coming," Harry said. "A lot of them."

"Good." Anselmo took another drink, then handed the bottle to Harry. "They will be a while—sorting this out."

THE din below ceased, replaced with the sounds of frightened horses and the voluble discourse of men. There were also a few moans and someone was screaming. This little battle had not been without casualties.

"What do you suppose is going on?" Anselmo asked.

"The American Civil War," said Harry.

And now another, closer sound. Voices, and a scraping against the cliff wall. Returning to the main chamber of the cave, they saw a man in a broad-brimmed hat, Union officer's jacket, and bright red sash ascend the ladder.

Harry lowered his pistol as the officer stepped into the cave. He studied them both, nodded to Anselmo, and then turned his attention to Harry.

"Senor Raines, so good to see you again."

"It is better to be seeing you, Colonel Chavez."

Chapter 27

"*ETES vous content, madame?*"

Were her dark eyes weapons, Harry would have been dead.

"*Je ne suis pas content,*" Madame Beignet said. "My leg is broken. I am being held against my wishes. You are stupid to ask me such a thing."

"*Je le regrette, madame.*" Harry leaned down and kissed her hand. She allowed it for a scant second, then snatched her hand away.

"I actually believed you," she said. "You are so Southern."

"Not Southern, ma'am. Virginian. We are our own place. And when this war and slavery are ended, I shall be residing there again."

"You will not live out this war, Raines. The Confederacy will hunt you down and kill you."

"I think the Union Army will give the Confederacy reason to be otherwise occupied. *Au revoir, madame.*"

She turned away from him on the narrow bed and lay

staring at the wall. Her injured leg was wrapped tightly in bandages. The other was shackled to the iron bed frame.

Stepping out of the tiny room, Harry moved aside as the guard relocked the door, then followed the man out onto the parade ground. Fort Marcy, situated on a bluff overlooking Santa Fe from the east, was a small post, with only a few buildings. They had accorded Madame Beignet the commandant's quarters, a privilege that did not sit well with many of the soldiers.

"How is she?" asked Colonel Weimers, when Harry rejoined him outside.

"Not happy."

"She's lucky to have come out of that little brawl with only a broken leg."

"I thought she'd been shot, when she went down. I didn't realize she had only stumbled on the rocks."

"Would have made things easier for me, were she to have perished. I don't know what to do with her. The manual prescribes hanging or a firing squad, but I don't know that the United States government has ever done that to a woman—no matter what their transgression."

They lighted cigars. Weimers started walking west toward the edge of the bluff. Harry followed, happy for the bath and change of clothes he'd enjoyed that day.

"You could deport her to the Confederacy," Harry said. "That's what President Lincoln decided to do with some female spies. Had them loaded onto a ship and sent into Dixie, so they'd be out of his hair."

"Trouble is, Madame Beignet's claiming French citizenship, and diplomatic immunity. Not clear what that's about, unless she's a French agent. I was sure she was a Rebel spy."

"It's all the same," Harry observed. "The French are interested in Mexico. The Confederates are interested in New Mexico. This *Liga de San Jeronimo* you and Colonel Chavez broke up was ready to stage a second Taos rebellion. The purposes of all three would have been served had it succeeded. The Union government would have been pushed out of here."

"We found twenty-four rifled muskets and four boxes of ammunition buried in her cellar. That would have been a start."

They reached the edge of the bluff. Marcy's two field howitzers commanded the entire town. Harry could make out the Almaden house, just past the plaza.

"I don't think they would have succeeded," Harry said.

"That's what they said about the Secessionists," said Weimers, eyeing the lack of polish on his boot. "A handful of states without a third of the North's population. No industry. No navy to speak of. Now we're into the second year of this damned war and getting pretty much nowhere."

"Not out here."

"No, that scuffle in Frijoles was their last gasp, though I doubt anyone's ever going to hear about it, let alone remember it for long."

"They'll remember Glorieta."

"No. Too much going on back East. We have labored in obscurity, Raines. I'm mentioning you in dispatches, though. We'd have had a hell of a mess on our hands if those San Jeronimo Mexicans had gotten all the arms they were after."

"I'd appreciate it, sir, if you didn't mention my name in dispatches. Or anywhere. Give the credit to Colonel Chavez. He's certainly earned it."

"You're sure?"

"Dispatches get read by a lot of people. Including some of the wrong ones."

"Very well. Your friends okay?"

"They are—unlike the unfortunate Roberto."

"Chavez tells me there wasn't a bullet in him. Just broke his head open in that fall."

"Casualties have been quite high in that family."

"Truly are an interesting mix of the good and the bad. That Anselmo, he's gone?"

"I believe that was his intent."

"Can't tell whether he's the good or the bad."

"I think he's the loyal." Harry turned back to the parade ground, where Tantou and Leahy were waiting with their horses.

"We'll be pulling out as soon as that column from California gets in," Weimers said. "Get back to Colorado as fast as we can. If the California boys get here in time, I could stick them with Madame Beignet."

"I think you should send her back to New Orleans. They say it's in Union hands now, but I don't think she knows that. It would be a surprise."

"She'd just run to the French consulate."

"What better place?"

Weimers paused. "You wouldn't want to wait a few days and take her with you?"

"That, sir, is the very last thing I'd like to do."

They walked a few more paces. "Your friend Leahy's going to go back with us?"

"He means to make his report, and he's convinced it's the fastest way East. Hook up with a railroad."

"Are you're still bent on going back through Texas?"

"I mean to get to New Orleans before that woman does."

"Just you and that Indian."

"That French Canadian. Yes."

"You're a braver man than I am, Raines."

"Not at all. Far from it. I just want to get home."

They joined the others. Harry climbed aboard One-Eye, taking the reins from Leahy.

"I will see you in Washington City, laddy buck," said the Irishman. "I trust you will not tarry."

"I'll buy you a drink in the bar of the National Hotel."

The teetotaling Leahy produced a mock frown. He knew very well it was a joke. Weimers came near again, putting a hand on One-Eye's neck.

"You think this creature'll make it that far down the Rio Grande?" Weimers asked.

"He's a surprise that way."

"Well, good-bye, then. I'd feel happier about your leaving if we'd been able to find that cache of gold you've been looking for."

"It'll turn up."

"I hope not in the form of rifles."

"I do not think that's a worry."

Tantou made a gentle clicking noise and his horse began to move off at a slow walk. Harry waved to Leahy and Weimers, then followed.

AT the rise southwest of Santa Fe on the Albuquerque road, Harry turned in his saddle to look back at the town.

"You sad to go, Harry Raines?"

"If she were there, I'd probably go right back."

"Not me."

"I'm surprised you didn't want to stay and wait for the soldiers from California."

"I can't, Harry Raines. Those soldiers know something about me."

"Something you haven't told me."

"The British are looking for me. The British in Canada."

"Have you broken one of their laws?"

"The Royal Canadian Mounted Police. I shot one of them at Fort Vancouver."

"Why?"

"He was going to shoot me. Or arrest me. Same result. I would have hanged."

They sat their horses, facing each other. "What did you do to make them want to do that?" Harry asked.

"I told you I am a Meti. They have made it very hard for us, and some of us have had enough. One day soon, we Meti are going to rise up, as those San Jeronimo people did at Taos. Only we will not fail."

Harry nudged One-Eye forward.

"Does that worry you, Harry Raines? You still want me to come with you?"

"I don't know how I'd make it without you."

Chapter 28

TANTOU had marked the shoes of Anselmo's horse in three places, making it as easy to track the man as it would have been had he lit bonfires every mile. Anslemo had a day's head start, however, and the others they were after, perhaps many days'.

Riding hard, they finally caught up with Anselmo on the morning of the fifth day, out on a desolate sweep of gray-brown ground well south of Peralta. The Mexican appeared to be tired and rode slowly, at a walk, hunched over as though asleep.

Tantou raised his hand, stopping. Anselmo was less than half a mile forward.

"If he sees us, then that is all there will be to this," Tantou said. "He will protect them to the end. By any means. He has shown us this."

"What do you suggest we do?"

"We let him go over the horizon, and then we stay with his track."

*   *   *

To either side of them, all over the landscape, were the mocking remnants of the Texans' putative conquest of New Mexico. The skeletal remains of dead horses and a few dead humans, broken wagons, discarded rifles, haversacks, cartridge boxes, and not a few household valuables, doubtless taken from the homes of the well-to-do in Santa Fe, lay scattered like detritus floating on the sea.

This time, Harry and Tantou ignored it all, pressing on doggedly, but slowly. Finally, ascending a long, low ridge at twilight, they saw in the flat valley beyond a campfire.

"It could be anyone," Tantou said.

"No. It must be them."

"That is wishing."

"Yes, but the feeling is strong."

"How should we come upon them? In the dark, someone might get shot."

"There are mountains ahead. They come down almost to the Rio Grande. I think we should go around these people and wait by those mountains. Take them by surprise, but quickly. So they do nothing bad to us."

Harry thought upon this. "That means riding all night."

"There is a moon."

"All right."

They found a place within a fold of boulders, close by both the Rio Grande and first rise of the mountains. The trail ran near. They slept until sunrise, then took positions and waited.

Tantou used his battered army field glasses.

"Here they come. Very slowly. Anselmo is with them."

"Let me see." Harry could not pick out that much detail, but he saw nothing to contradict Tantou's assessment.

"We must be careful to let them get a little way past us and take them from the rear," Tantou said. "I believe that Anselmo would shoot us if we give him a chance."

"No, Jack. I want to do it this way." Harry moved One-Eye out onto the trail.

THE three of them came steady on. Harry looked to his left, where he saw that Tantou had taken a position some one fifty yards distant—far enough away to assure that no gun could be trained on the both of them, yet close enough for Tantou to fire to good effect. He had his rifle out of its scabbard and sat quietly in the saddle with a patience Harry could not share.

The wagon drew up just within pistol range of Harry. It was heavily loaded with what looked to be household goods and carried a man and a woman, sitting close together in the seat.

Anselmo spurred his horse forward and came up to Harry at a jingling trot. Tantou could have shot him easily from his position, but Anselmo paid no mind to that possibility.

He came up very close. "Don Luis wants to know if you mean to bar his passage," Anselmo asked.

"No. I am here to settle a curiosity. I want to know if what he carries is the gold that was given to the *Liga de San Jeronimo*."

Anselmo looked at him as he might some strange and peculiar object on exhibition. "You know that it is."

"And he takes it to Mexico? Not Texas."

"He does. It is long overdue."

"To Benito Juárez?"

"*Sí.*"

"That is United States gold—I believe seized unlawfully by the Secessionists in Texas when they took over."

"This gold comes from the French woman. I don't know where she got it, but it doesn't matter to us. What matters is where it goes."

"What will you do with it?"

"We will use it to help Presidente Benito Juárez defend his government against his enemies. You know all this, Raines."

The wind had picked up and was whipping great bundles of weeds across the arid plain. It caused cloth to wave and flutter from the wagon.

"I will talk to them."

DON Luis kept a rifle aimed at Harry from the moment he left Anselmo until he pulled One-Eye up abreast of the wagon. Isabel was almost lost within the hood of her cloak—and deliberately kept her eyes from his.

"I promised your daughter I would find out who killed you, Don Luis," said Harry. "But here you are, very much alive."

The older man sat unmoving on his seat. He had a sort of blanket over his shoulders—what the Mexicans called a serape.

"I mean you no harm, Don Luis. I know what you are carrying in your wagon. I will not stand in your way."

The wind rose, blowing back Isabel's hood. He could fully see her face now, but not tell her mood.

Her father seemed much the same man as in his photograph, but not so vigorous. Weary, he was, and melancholy.

"I would like to speak to your daughter. Then I will go."

"Very well. Speak."

"No. I mean alone." He looked back toward the boulders where he and Tantou had waited. "Over there."

No one spoke or moved. At last, with only a glance to her father, Isabel turned and stepped down to the ground. She stood there stoically, as though about to endure some punishment. Her hair was loose, and the wind blew it about her face.

Harry dismounted and started toward the rocks. She followed. When he stopped, it was at a place where they could be clearly seen from the wagon, but not heard. She came slowly to him, stopping close enough for her cloak to brush his hand when the wind blew it.

"That is your brother Eduardo in your father's grave at Glorieta," he said, stating fact, not posing a question.

"Sadly, yes. Though I am happy it is not my father." She shifted her eyes to the wagon. Anselmo was riding slowly back toward it. "How did you know this?"

"That was the only thing I clearly understood at first. There was a round shotgun pattern in the wall, indicating a clear miss. It went high, hitting no one. There were some shotgun pellets in the floor, on the other side of the desk from where your father was sitting. As I later discovered at Glorieta, that man they struck was already dead. He'd been shot in the back first. With a pistol."

She shuddered, despite herself.

"Anselmo is a very loyal man," Harry said. "I presume he was the one with the pistol."

"No. Eduardo was killed by Roberto. He shot him when

he saw that Eduardo meant to kill our father. He so loved my father that he would kill his own brother. And he did. Then he ran away. He came back when he thought it was safe."

"He wasn't trying to take the gold?"

"They all were—Roberto, Eduardo, my cousin Alejandro. But Roberto would never harm my father. He would never trade my father's life for gold."

"Not so Eduardo."

"No. Eduardo and Alejandro, they became very bad men."

"And the shotgun?"

"That was Anselmo's idea. He saw it as a way for my father to escape these people and get the gold to Benito Juárez. To bury Eduardo in my father's place."

"And Senor Martinez and his wife? Pablo Sanchez?"

"I don't know who did that but I know it was not Roberto."

"As it turns out, that is the truth. Best I can determine, it was Alejandro's pistol that killed those poor people."

"How do you know that?"

Harry took some of the spent bullets he'd collected in his pocket and held them out to her in his open hand. "There is a way to tell these things, from the bullets."

Gingerly, she picked one up, looking at it closely, not comprehending. "I do not understand." She dropped it back with the others.

"It doesn't matter. There'll be no trial. There's no need for such evidence." Harry dug all of the bullets out and tossed them onto the sandy ground.

"How did my brother Roberto die?" Her voice was very cold and dry, in keeping with the land around them.

"He fell from the cliff at Frijoles Canyon."

"That is not the truth."

"He had help in his fall."

"Who?"

"Jack Tantou."

"Why would he do that?"

"He told me afterward that Roberto was about to shoot Madame Beignet, and Tantou thought she was more valuable to us in the Union than Roberto."

"Could he not have simply disarmed him?"

"He said that is what he tried to do, in that very small space. But your brother was young and very strong and fought. That is how he fell. His revolver went off, and he hit Emiliano Vasquez instead of Madame Beignet."

"If someone had shot her two months ago we would have all been spared much misery."

"That's of little help now."

"You people, North and South, you shouldn't have brought your war here. It doesn't belong."

"There are those who would not have it anywhere, but I am grateful that it carried me to you."

She turned, looking to her father.

"They were rough boys, Eduardo and Alejandro," she said. "But not all bad. That gold turned them into something worse."

"Why did your father give Martinez and your brother chests that contained nothing but rocks and iron?"

"He did not trust them. He gave gold only to Senor Sanchez, who was a Juárez man."

"He has trusted you."

"Yes. Me and Anselmo. And that's how we come to where we are this day."

"And you're going to Mexico."

"If we can."

He took a step closer to her and, sensing it to be right, put his arms around her shoulders. She did not try to back away. Instead, she tilted back her head and looked straight up into the very pure and flawless blue sky, as though seeing something in it he could not. Then, to his surprise, she turned around and kissed him and held him as tightly as she could. The wind came at them again, her hair blowing around his head and face. Then it relented, and so did she.

"I did not come to you that night to distract you from our plans," she said. "I came because I did not think that such a time would come again."

"But here we are."

"You could come with us," she said. "To Mexico. There are gringos with Juárez, and you are very clever. You would be of great help. And it is the same cause. The enemy is the same. His opponents have made slaves of the peons, of the Indians. Tantou as well. The both of you could come."

"If I came, it would be because of you—not Juárez. Not the peons."

"Then come for me."

ALMADEN sat coldly in his seat on the wagon, his eyes steady on his daughter and the place where she stood talking to the gringo. She had talked to him about this man. Though she did not say so, it seemed very clear to him that this Raines was someone she might well marry.

He was a good man, apparently, and working in a good cause, but Almaden could think of no eventuality he might loathe more. Isabel was a daughter of Mexico as much as she was of his, and it was to a Mexican life they were bound. Raines would take her away from that, remove her to far away Virginia or someplace worse—transform her as so many women of Santa Fe had been transformed, turn her into another Alicia Montebello.

He had lost his sons. Now he would lose her. It was too great a price. The United States government was obligated to him for what had been gained at Glorieta. Instead, it was making him pay.

Almaden raised his rifle to his shoulder, propping his elbow on his knee. He squinted down the barrel. There was wind to adjust for, but the range was no problem.

"Senor," said Anselmo.

"Yes?"

"You could kill her."

"No. I would save her."

"Either way, you would lose her."

Almaden kept his eye upon the sights, then finally, unhappily, lifted his head and lowered the rifle.

"Again, Anselmo. You are right."

He watched as she kissed the gringo once again, holding him more closely than Almaden had seen her with any man—even her own brothers, even him. She stayed like that for the longest time. He had a compulsion to bring the rifle to bear again—not to shoot, perhaps, but to make her see it.

He did not. Slowly, Isabel withdrew from the man, then turned and, head down, started walking slowly back toward the wagon.

Raines remained where he was.

* * *

ANSELMO dismounted to help her back into the wagon, then slapped Raines's horse on the rump, sending it back toward its owner.

Almaden put his arm around his daughter. She did not resist, but she did not move closer.

"Are you very sad, daughter?"

"Yes. Very sad."

"You will continue on with me?"

"I will."

"You rejected him, then?" He flicked the reins, and the team lurched the wagon forward.

"No, father. But let us talk no more of this."

HARRY did not look back until he and Tantou had ridden to the next rise in the trail. The wagon was under way, but moving slowly, and far behind them now.

"She asked you to come with them?" Tantou said.

"Yes. You, too."

"But you said no."

"Almost didn't."

"So now you will be unhappy."

"Yes. But maybe I will have a happy memory."

"A poor substitute, Harry Raines."

"Perhaps I will come back."

"But not soon."

"No. Not soon. Not soon at all. After the war."